Teen Depression

Titles in the Diseases & Disorders series include:

Acne
ADHD
Alcoholism
Allergies
Alzheimer's Disease
Amnesia
Anorexia and Bulimia
Anxiety Disorders
Asperger's Syndrome
Asthma
Autism
Autoimmune Disorders
Blindness
Brain Trauma
Brain Tumors
Breast Cancer
Cancer
Cerebral Palsy
Cervical Cancer
Childhood Obesity
Cystic Fibrosis
Dementia
Depression
Diabetes
Epilepsy
Exercise Addiction
Fibromyalgia
Growth Disorders

Hepatitis
Human Papillomavirus (HPV)
Infectious Mononucleosis
Leukemia
Lyme Disease
Malnutrition
Mental Retardation
Migraines
MRSA
Multiple Sclerosis
Osteoporosis
Personality Disorders
Phobias
Plague
Post Traumatic Stress
   Disorder
Prostate Cancer
Radiation Sickness
Sexually Transmitted
   Diseases
Skin Cancer
Speech Disorders
Sports Injuries
Sudden Infant Death
   Syndrome
Thyroid Disorders
Tourette Syndrome
West Nile Virus

DISEASES & DISORDERS

Teen Depression

Peggy J. Parks

LUCENT BOOKS

A part of Gale, Cengage Learning

GALE
CENGAGE Learning

Detroit • New York • San Francisco • New Haven, Conn • Waterville, Maine • London

© 2013 Gale, Cengage Learning

LIBRARY OF CONGRESS CATALOGING-IN-PUBLICATION DATA

Parks, Peggy J., 1951-
  Teen depression / by Peggy J. Parks.
      p. cm. -- (Diseases & disorders)
  Includes bibliographical references and index.
  ISBN 978-1-4205-0837-6 (hardcover)
  1. Depression in adolescence--Juvenile literature. I. Title.
  RJ506.D4.P373 2013
  616.85'2700835--dc23

                                                        2012028092

Lucent Books
27500 Drake Rd.
Farmington Hills, MI 48331

ISBN-13: 978-1-4205-0837-6
ISBN-10: 1-4205-0837-7

Printed in the United States of America
1 2 3 4 5 6 7 16 15 14 13 12

Table of Contents

"The Most Difficult Puzzles Ever Devised"

Charles Best, one of the pioneers in the search for a cure for diabetes, once explained what it is about medical research that intrigued him so. "It's not just the gratification of knowing one is helping people," he confided, "although that probably is a more heroic and selfless motivation. Those feelings may enter in, but truly, what I find best is the feeling of going toe to toe with nature, of trying to solve the most difficult puzzles ever devised. The answers are there somewhere, those keys that will solve the puzzle and make the patient well. But how will those keys be found?"

Since the dawn of civilization, nothing has so puzzled people—and often frightened them, as well—as the onset of illness in a body or mind that had seemed healthy before. A seizure, the inability of a heart to pump, the sudden deterioration of muscle tone in a small child—being unable to reverse such conditions or even to understand why they occur was unspeakably frustrating to healers. Even before there were names for such conditions, even before they were understood at all, each was a reminder of how complex the human body was, and how vulnerable.

While our grappling with understanding diseases has been frustrating at times, it has also provided some of humankind's most heroic accomplishments. Alexander Fleming's accidental discovery in 1928 of a mold that could be turned into penicillin has resulted in the saving of untold millions of lives. The isolation of the enzyme insulin has reversed what was once a death sentence for anyone with diabetes. There have been great strides in combating conditions for which there is not yet a cure, too. Medicines can help AIDS patients live longer, diagnostic tools such as mammography and ultrasounds can help doctors find tumors while they are treatable, and laser surgery techniques have made the most intricate, minute operations routine.

This "toe-to-toe" competition with diseases and disorders is even more remarkable when seen in a historical continuum. An astonishing amount of progress has been made in a very short time. Just two hundred years ago, the existence of germs as a cause of some diseases was unknown. In fact, it was less than 150 years ago that a British surgeon named Joseph Lister had difficulty persuading his fellow doctors that washing their hands before delivering a baby might increase the chances of a healthy delivery (especially if they had just attended to a diseased patient)!

Each book in Lucent's Diseases and Disorders series explores a disease or disorder and the knowledge that has been accumulated (or discarded) by doctors through the years. Each book also examines the tools used for pinpointing a diagnosis, as well as the various means that are used to treat or cure a disease. Finally, new ideas are presented—techniques or medicines that may be on the horizon.

Frustration and disappointment are still part of medicine, for not every disease or condition can be cured or prevented. But the limitations of knowledge are being pushed outward constantly; the "most difficult puzzles ever devised" are finding challengers every day.

Trapped in Darkness

As contrary as it may seem, the teenage years can be a fun, happy time in someone's life and also a very difficult time. The changes that occur during puberty affect the minds of young people as well as their bodies, which means that moodiness and feeling down is a normal part of growing up. These periods of sadness, anger, and confusion usually pass within a couple of days, and the teen feels much better. But the illness known as depression goes far beyond normal teenage blues. It is a serious medical condition that is characterized by feelings of deep sadness, hopelessness, and the sense that life no longer has any meaning. Therapeutic consultant Dore Frances explains: "Occasional bad moods or acting out is to be expected, yet depression is something different. Depression can destroy the very essence of a teenager's personality, causing an overwhelming sense of sadness, despair, or anger."[1] Unlike normal bouts of gloominess, the sadness associated with depression does not fade away—it can last for weeks, months, and even years.

"Loneliness Haunted Me"

The deep, lingering sadness of depression is often confusing for teens who suffer from it. They cannot understand why they hurt so much, why they do not feel happy like their friends do, and why activities they used to enjoy are not fun anymore. Coping with this day after day can be unbearable, as Olivia Thompson knows. A pretty, popular teenager from Comstock Park, Michigan, Olivia had a variety of interests, including photography, basketball, and listening to music. She also volunteered her time to work at the local humane society, where she loved playing with the puppies and other animals. That all changed in January 2011, when she suddenly felt as though a curtain of darkness had fallen over her. "I realized something was wrong with me," Olivia says. "I started feeling sad and helpless." She withdrew from her friends, quit the middle school basketball team, wanted only to be alone, and spent hours crying in her bedroom. "Loneliness haunted me," she says. "I felt hollow inside. I could be in a crowded room and still feel lonely."[2]

Olivia instinctively knew that what she was feeling was not normal, so she talked to her parents about it. She asked to have a mental health evaluation, only to be disheartened by a psychologist who dismissed her feelings as just part of being a teenager. Olivia knew that assumption was wrong, however, because of how badly she was suffering. "A week later, I couldn't take it anymore," she says. "I just laid in my bed. I was crying so hard."[3] Olivia's mother took her to a mental health facility, where she was diagnosed with major depression. She was given prescription medications and admitted to the facility for two weeks of group and individual counseling. To her great relief, she soon began to feel better.

Even though light was finally starting to pierce the darkness, Olivia's progress was overshadowed by what she encountered after returning to school. She says that kids treated her like she was crazy, with some avoiding her altogether and others making fun of her. "Everybody looked at me like I was a monster," says Olivia. "They either talked to me like I was a 4-year-old or like I was going to hurt them. It was heartbreaking. I was horrified to walk down the hall."[4]

As hurtful as that experience was, Olivia refused to let it defeat her. With the support of her family, combined with the strength and healing she had gained from her counseling sessions,

Depression goes far beyond normal teenage blues. It is a serious medical condition characterized by feelings of deep sadness, hopelessness, and a sense that life no longer has any meaning.

she overcame depression. In September 2011 she started a new high school filled with optimism and hope, along with a new-found resolve to find ways of helping other teenagers who suffer from depression. She began to study neuropsychology, which is a branch of psychology that involves understanding the relationship between the brain, thinking, and behavior. Says Olivia: "Someday I want to be the one to help explain to kids what's going on in their brains making them sad."[5]

Silent Suffering

Olivia was fortunate because she realized that something was seriously wrong and reached out for help. The unfortunate reality, however, is that most depressed teenagers never tell anyone how badly they are hurting; instead, they keep their feelings to themselves. Mental health experts say that there are a number of reasons for this, such as young people wrongly assuming that depression symptoms are just part of being an adolescent. Others are hesitant to seek mental health care because of what their peers might think of them, or they would like to seek help but have no idea where to go for it. As a result, the majority of teens with depression do not receive treatment—which means they live with constant emotional pain and misery.

As bleak as the situation may seem, there is good news: Like Olivia, young people who are treated for depression have an excellent chance of overcoming it. Also, awareness of adolescent depression has grown in recent years, with increasing numbers of people realizing that it is a serious illness, rather than just a form of teenage moodiness. Mental health organizations and advocacy groups have called for significantly increased efforts to identify depression in teenagers through routine screenings, which could help catch the illness at an early stage. In the future, as more depressed teens are identified and treated, fewer will have to endure this devastating illness. For those who do suffer from it, Olivia offers a message of hope: "There's help. You're not alone."[6]

CHAPTER ONE

What Is Depression?

Teenagers often experience mood swings that cause them to feel fantastic one day and miserable the next. As frustrating as this can be, most young people find that the good things about life far outweigh the bad—unless they suffer from depression. For many depressed teens, good days are rare or even nonexistent. Sometimes they feel so overwhelmed by emotional pain that they dread getting up in the morning, as though just making it through the day is too much to face. In *The Depression Answer Book*, author and psychiatrist Wes Burgess says that depression can cause someone's whole view of life to be distorted. He writes: "Your mind is taken over by worries, self-criticism, guilt, and thoughts of death. . . . Good situations look worse than they are, and bad situations look hopeless. Wherever you look, there is no satisfaction and no peace from your dark, negative emotions and thoughts."[7] This sense of hopelessness is characteristic of depression, which is why it causes such misery for teens who suffer from it.

"No Trendy Diagnosis"

Depression is a mood disorder, part of a group of mental illnesses that involve severe disturbances in a person's emotional state, or mood. This categorization is often a source of confusion, as it can cause people to assume that having depression is the same as being in a "bad mood"—but nothing could be further from the truth. Burgess explains: "After all, if you're just in a bad mood, people wonder why you cannot exert some effort and pull yourself out of it. However, you usually cannot pull yourself out of major depression; it can be severely debilitating."[8]

Depression is one of the oldest known medical conditions, an illness that scientists have been aware of, and curious about, for hundreds of years. Says Burgess: "Depression is no trendy diagnosis; we have known about it and been aware of its seriousness for a long time."[9] As far back as the fifth century B.C., the renowned physician Hippocrates, whom Burgess refers to as "the Greek godfather of medicine,"[10] described depressive symptoms such as sleeplessness, irritability, sadness, restlessness, and diminished appetite. Hippocrates was one of the first great thinkers to assert that depression was a genuine illness, rather than an imagined malady, and that it affected the body as well as the mind. Centuries later, British scholar Robert Burton wrote a book called *The Anatomy of Melancholy*, which was published in 1621. One of the first English-language volumes about depression, it discussed a number of scientific theories and also drew on Burton's personal experience with the illness. In the years following the publication of these early writings, countless others wrote about depression, and this helped scientists gain a better understanding of it.

Yet even with awareness of depression rooted in ancient writings, it was not until the mid-twentieth century that scientists realized the illness was not unique to adults. Prior to that time, the prevailing assumption among those in the medical field was that children and adolescents could not suffer from depression. Because their brains were still maturing, depressive symptoms were thought to be a result of normal developmental processes. The National Institute of Mental Health (NIMH) explains: "Teens with depression were often dismissed as being moody or difficult."[11] Perceptions about who could be affected by depression began to change during the late 1970s. A few researchers rejected the theory that it was solely an adult disease and established that the illness could indeed affect

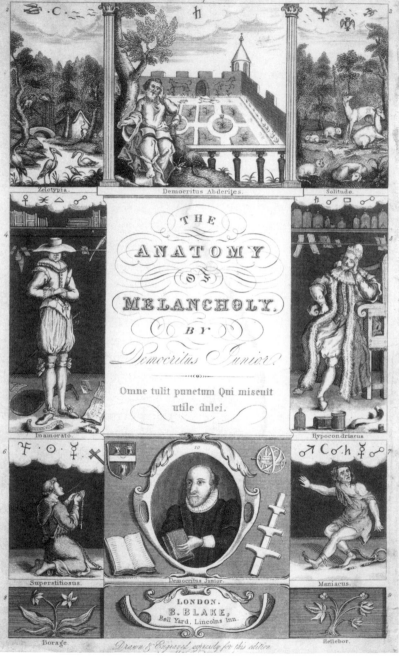

Robert Burton's 1621 book *The Anatomy of Melancholy* was one of the first English-language books to address depression from a scientific perspective.

young people as well as old. During this time, depression was also shown to cause symptoms in children and adolescents that were essentially the same as those seen in adults. This change in viewpoint led to the American Psychiatric Association's (APA) revising criteria for depression in its *Diagnostic and Statistical Manual of Mental Disorders*, which is commonly referred to as the DSM. In its 1980 edition, the DSM clearly stated that depression could begin at any age, and subsequent versions of the manual continued to reflect that.

Symptoms and Levels of Severity

The latest edition of the DSM is the fourth revision, the DSM-IV-TR, which was released in July 2000 and includes sixteen major diagnostic classes. Within the mood disorders category is depressive disorders, along with nine characterizing symptoms established by the APA. These include feeling sad or irritable most of the day, nearly every day; a loss of interest in or enjoyment of most or all activities; increased or decreased appetite accompanied by significant weight gain or loss; sleeping too much or not being able to sleep; slowed thinking or functioning that is obvious to others; constantly feeling tired and having little energy; feelings of guilt, self-blame, and worthlessness; trouble concentrating and making decisions; and a preoccupation with death and dying, including suicidal thoughts and/or a suicide attempt. Because no two cases of depression are exactly the same, not everyone who has the illness exhibits all symptoms listed in the DSM. Says the National Alliance on Mental Illness (NAMI): "For example, someone may have problems with his or her sleep and feel low in energy, but find that appetite remains normal."[12]

Sleeping problems are one of the most common warning signs that a teen suffers from depression. Since adolescents naturally require more sleep than adults, it can be easy for parents to mistake this for normal teenage behavior. The difference, however, is that depressed teens feel exhausted most of the time, even after sleeping soundly for eight hours or more, and they cannot seem to get enough sleep. No matter how much sleep they get, they still feel exhausted and drained of energy.

Of the nine characteristic depressive disorder symptoms established by the American Psychiatric Association, a problem sleeping is one of the most common warning signs of teen depression.

There are several varieties of depression, and the type that someone is diagnosed with depends on the number of symptoms and the severity of impairment. The most severe type is major depression, which is also called major depressive disorder or clinical depression. Teens who have major depression exhibit five or more symptoms nearly every day for two weeks or longer, with at least one of the symptoms being a depressed mood or a loss of interest in or pleasure from favorite activities. This is depression at its very worst, an illness that causes so much pain and misery for those who suffer from it that they may wonder whether life is even worth living. Such was the case with Emily Fagan, a teenager from Aurora, Illinois. Formerly happy, energetic, and involved in numerous school activities, in 2009 she was stricken with such severe depression that she spent most of her time crying or sleeping. "I was in so much intense pain," she says. One day while riding in the car with her mother, Emily was suddenly overcome with despair and broke down. "I just lost it," she says. "I started crying and couldn't stop. I was feeling like, 'I hate myself, I hate school, I hate everything.'"[13]

Not all forms of depression cause symptoms as severe as Emily's. Minor depression, for example, is a milder form of the illness that is diagnosed when someone exhibits two or more of the APA's criteria for at least two weeks. Closely related is dysthymic disorder, which is also known as dysthymia. Diagnostic criteria are the same as for minor depression (at least two symptoms), but dysthymia is a chronic illness, meaning that it lasts for a long time. Teens who suffer from it experience symptoms for a year or two, and sometimes even longer, which can be extremely distressing for them. According to the

Dysthymic teens often feel irritable, suffer from poor concentration and indecisiveness, and experience periods of hopelessness.

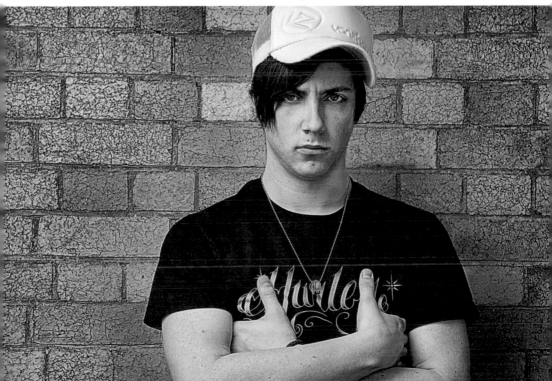

American Academy of Child & Adolescent Psychiatry, dysthymic teens often feel irritable, have low self-esteem, suffer from poor concentration and indecisiveness, and have periods of feeling hopeless. The group writes: "This chronically depressed mood colors every experience, impression, and response, and the teen experiences most things negatively."[14]

Sporadic Depression

In addition to the primary forms of depression (major, minor, and dysthymia), some types affect individuals only under certain circumstances. One example is postpartum depression, a condition that usually develops within four to eight weeks of having a baby. Postpartum depression differs from what mental health professionals call the baby blues, which is a heightened emotional state that causes many new mothers to feel sad, tearful, afraid, and anxious. Those symptoms can also signify postpartum depression—but postpartum depression is much more severe and long lasting. The National Institutes of Health (NIH) explains: "Postpartum depression can make you feel restless, anxious, fatigued and worthless. Some new moms worry they will hurt themselves or their babies. Unlike the 'baby blues,' postpartum depression does not go away quickly."[15]

The National Institutes of Health says that hundreds of thousands of new mothers experience postpartum depression, with the highest risk among teenage moms. According to the Centers for Disease Control and Prevention, teenagers who have given birth have a much greater chance of developing postpartum depression than older mothers, largely because of the drastic changes in their lives after a baby is born. Due to their young age, teenage girls who are faced with being parents can be overwhelmed by the responsibility and stress. A life that was once carefree, filled with social activities and hanging out with friends, suddenly revolves around caring for a tiny infant. These changes, combined with the extreme hormonal changes that take place during pregnancy, can lead to severe postpartum depression in teenage mothers.

Another type of depression, known as seasonal affective disorder (SAD), develops during certain times of the year. It is sometimes called winter depression because most cases strike during the winter months when sunlight is diminished, the weather is cold, and the skies are dreary and gray. Studies of people who suffer from SAD have shown that it is most common among young adults, but teenagers can develop it, too. Its severity can vary from person to person, as a January 2009 article on the health information site WebMD explains: "Some

Sarah's Battle

A young woman named Sarah began to struggle with depression when she was fifteen years old, and she spoke frankly about it during an August 31, 2009, interview:

Around 15 is when I can best remember starting to feel "less happy" or numb. I remember thinking one day . . . shouldn't I be enjoying this more? I was hanging out with friends and everyone was laughing and having a great time, but I caught myself laughing because that's what everyone else was doing. But I wasn't finding anything funny. . . . Then I started to recognize other symptoms. I was numb to everything. I found it hard to bring myself out of bed, I wasn't hungry, I couldn't bring myself to enjoy things I normally did. At first I had no clue what was going on, I felt confused. I thought maybe it's just me going through a phase, but the feelings never left. It honestly felt like I was sinking in a pit of sand that was 1000 pounds heavy, but I couldn't get myself out, and I didn't want to. People say, "Well just change how you think about things, let the little things go," or my favorite, "It's not that bad. Think about how much pain other people are in." Well, when [you're] that depressed you can't. You can't see other people's pain because yours is so great. People who don't suffer from depression need to understand that you have to measure your own pain with your own measuring stick. Everyone is different.

Sarah, interviewed by Teri Robert. "Teen Depression—an Interview." My Depression Connection, HealthCentral, August 31, 2009. www.healthcentral.com/depression /teens-304402-5_pf.html.

teens with SAD have very mild symptoms and just feel out-of-sorts or irritable. Others have more serious symptoms that interfere with relationships and schoolwork."[16] In most cases of SAD, symptoms start out relatively mild and then become progressively worse as the season wears on.

One teenager, called "Claire," experienced this form of depression when she was diagnosed with SAD at the age of fifteen. When school started in the fall, she was excited about making new friends and had all sorts of plans for her sophomore year, including being part of the school newspaper staff. Then as it got closer to winter, Claire found that no matter how long she slept, she was exhausted and drained of energy, and she began to feel moody and depressed much of the time. Normally enthusiastic about writing, she could not concentrate on her articles and started missing deadlines. Her friends stopped calling her because of how drastically her personality had changed. When Claire was not invited to sit with them at football games or was left out of fun events like weekend sleepovers, she sank even deeper into depression. Finally, a doctor diagnosed her with SAD and helped her begin the road to recovery.

Intense Highs and Lows

Bipolar disorder (originally called manic depression) is a mood disorder, and it is often associated with depression because sufferers go through depressed periods known as "episodes." Since the two conditions are closely related, they were often believed to be the same illness. As psychologist John M. Grohol points out: "That's one of the reasons manic depression's clinical name changed to 'bipolar disorder' many years ago, to more clearly distinguish it from regular depression."[17] Since depressive episodes are a key element of bipolar disorder, many who suffer from it are initially diagnosed with depression. Their illness, however, involves more than phases of being severely depressed. Teens with bipolar disorder also have bouts of exaggerated euphoria and excitability, which are known as manic episodes or mania. According to the NIMH, each depressive or manic episode can last for a week or two, and sometimes longer.

During manic episodes, teens become hyperactive, overly excited, and "wired." Their minds start racing uncontrollably, causing them to talk very fast about many different topics at once without making much sense. They may act happy and silly in a way that is not normal for them or become easily agitated, perhaps displaying explosive outbursts of temper. It is also common during manic episodes for teens to use poor judgment and engage in risky behaviors. The NIMH explains: "Sometimes behavior problems go along with mood episodes.

Manic depression is now called bipolar disorder to better distinguish it from clinical depression.

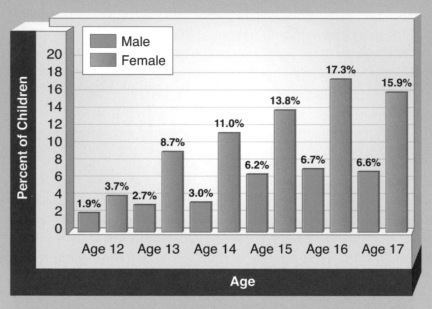

Occurrence of Major Depressive Episode (MDE)* Among Adolescents Aged 12–17 Years in the Past Year, by Age and Gender, 2007

Percent of Children

- Male
- Female

Age 12: 1.9%, 3.7%
Age 13: 2.7%, 8.7%
Age 14: 3.0%, 11.0%
Age 15: 6.2%, 13.8%
Age 16: 6.7%, 17.3%
Age 17: 6.6%, 15.9%

Age

*MDE is defined as a period of at least two weeks when a person experienced a depressed mood or loss of pleasure in daily activities and had a majority of specific depression symptoms.

Taken from: Substance Abuse and Mental Health Services Administration, National Survey of Drug Use and Health. www.mibba.com/articles/health/3291/teen-depression-fact-vs-fiction/.

Young people may take a lot of risks, like drive too fast or spend too much money."[18] Bipolar disorder can also cause affected teens to have suicidal thoughts.

The most serious form of bipolar disorder is known as type I. According to the NIMH, those with bipolar disorder type I may have such severe manic episodes that they need immediate hospital care. Another type, one that is milder, is bipolar disorder II. This illness causes depressive symptoms, but rather than having full manic episodes, sufferers experience a milder form of mania known as hypomania. The NAMI explains, though, that a hypomanic episode may be a sign that a severe manic episode is about to follow, "or it may be a sign that a person is going to 'crash' and become depressed."[19]

Hypomania is also a characteristic of a milder form of bipolar disorder known as cyclothymic disorder. Teens with this illness experience moods that are abnormally high or low at least half of the time, but the mood swings are less severe than with full-blown bipolar disorder. The Mayo Clinic explains: "When you have cyclothymia, you can typically function in your daily life, though not always well. The unpredictable nature of your mood shifts may significantly disrupt your life because you never know how you're going to feel—and you can't just will yourself to live life on an even keel."[20]

Who Suffers from Depression?

The exact prevalence of mood disorders among teens is unknown because symptoms are often confused with normal personality changes that occur during adolescence. With depression, for instance, teens themselves often do not know that something is wrong. Adolescent psychologist Lisa Boesky explains: "Even if you ask them straight out, 'are you depressed?,' they don't recognize it even in themselves. And a lot of parents don't recognize it."[21] Because symptoms often go unreported, or are unnoticed by depressed individuals or the people around them, the majority of teens who have depression are never diagnosed. This was one of the findings of a 2009 study of adolescents by psychiatrists from India, who discovered that primary care physicians failed to recognize depression in as many as half of the teens who consulted with them. In the absence of exact numbers, health officials can only make estimates about the prevalence of youth depression. In a 2011 report, the Federal Interagency Forum on Child and Family Statistics estimates that depression affects 8 percent of youth aged twelve to seventeen.

Although it affects teens of both genders, depression is believed to be much more common among females than males. The Harvard Medical School explains: "Before puberty, neither sex has the edge on major depression, but afterward girls are two to

three times more likely than boys to suffer from it."[22] This dispar-
ity is puzzling to scientists, but research has suggested several
possible reasons for it. One theory is that dramatic hormonal
changes during puberty increase the risk of depression. These
changes affect both males and females, but the higher prevalence of depression among teenage girls has led scientists to
question whether the illness is somehow related to their hormonal fluctuations.

Another possible reason for the higher depression prevalence among teenage girls involves psychological differences
between them and their male peers. The NIMH says that after
adolescent girls have experienced difficult situations or
events, they are more likely than boys to continue feeling bad
rather than getting over it, which suggests that girls may be
more prone to developing depression. The NIMH's conclusion
is based on a study published in the April 2005 issue of the
Journal of Abnormal Child Psychology, which found a strong
tendency among young girls to doubt themselves, question their
problem-solving abilities, and view their problems as unsolv-
able, more so than was characteristic of boys. Says the NIMH:
"The girls with these views were more likely to have depressive
symptoms. . . . Girls also tended to need a higher degree of ap-
proval and success to feel secure than boys."[23]

Coexisting Illnesses

Teenagers with depression often suffer from one or more ac-
companying mental health disorders, a condition known as co-
morbidity. This coexisting of illnesses is extremely common
among depressed teens, as psychologists Cecilia A. Essau and
Weining C. Chang explain: "Comorbidity is so common that it
is regarded as the rule rather than the exception."[24] According
to the NIMH, the most common mental illnesses that co-occur
with depression are anxiety disorders, which involve intense,
overpowering feelings of anxiety that are typically based on irrational fears and dread. The anxiety disorders that typically
accompany depression are obsessive-compulsive disorder,
panic disorder, social phobia, generalized anxiety disorder, and
post-traumatic stress disorder (PTSD).

The latter has been shown to be one of the most psychologically devastating mental illnesses for people of all ages. PTSD develops after someone has experienced a terrifying, life-changing event or ordeal. Teenagers who suffer from it were likely exposed as children to one or more traumatic events that evoked intense fear, helplessness, and/or horror. Psychiatrist Roy H. Lubit explains: "Traumatic events can take many forms, including physical or sexual assaults, natural disasters, traumatic death of a loved one, or emotional abuse or neglect."[25] The strong link between teen depression and PTSD was revealed during a 2009 study known as the Teen Depression Awareness Project, which

The most common mental illness to co-occur with depression is anxiety disorder, the symptoms of which include intense feelings of anxiety rooted in irrational fear and dread.

Depressed and Terrified

Depression causes numerous problems for teens who suffer from it—and for those with psychotic depression, life can be a nightmare. This severe form of depression is characterized by psychosis, which is the state of being out of touch with reality. James C. Overholser, who is a professor of psychology and the director of clinical training at Case Western Reserve University in Cleveland, Ohio, explains: "Psychotic depression is a relatively rare condition that occurs when someone displays both severe depression and a break with reality. The loss of contact with reality may take the form of delusions, hallucinations, or thought disorders."

Delusions are strange, irrational beliefs that have no basis in reality, while hallucinations involve hearing or seeing things that do not actually exist. During a psychotic episode, teens may hear voices telling them what to do, or be haunted by strange and illogical ideas, such as being convinced that their friends can hear their thoughts. They may also believe that friends and family members are involved in an elaborate plot to harm them. In many cases teens with psychotic depression know that these feelings and thoughts are not real, but they feel powerless to stop them—and are often too ashamed to tell anyone how much they are suffering.

Quoted in Chris Iliades. "Psychotic Depression: Losing Touch with Reality." EverydayHealth.com, September 8, 2011. www.everyday health.com/depression/psychotic-depression-losing-touch-with-reality.aspx.

People with psychotic depression are out of touch with reality and experience delusions, hallucinations, and thought disorders.

was conducted by psychologists from the nonprofit research firm the Rand Corporation. The study involved nearly four hundred teens from Los Angeles, California, and Washington, D.C., with roughly half of the participants suffering from depression. The psychologists found that of the depressed teens, over 60 percent had also been diagnosed with PTSD.

Crushed Hopes and Dreams

Depression has long been recognized as a serious mental illness, but only since the 1970s have scientists known that it affects teenagers as well as adults. Because its symptoms can resemble typical adolescent moodiness, depression often goes undiagnosed—which means that those who suffer from it often live in a constant state of emotional turmoil. Although its symptoms vary from mild to severe, any form of depression can be distressing for teens. It can skew their thoughts, rob them of their dreams, and cause them to view the future, and even life itself, as grim, bleak, and hopeless.

CHAPTER TWO

Causes of Depression in Teens

Scientists have successfully identified an exact cause for many diseases and disorders, but this is not true for depression. It remains a puzzling illness, one that is thought to result from a complex interaction of genetic, biological, and environmental factors. This combination of causes is discussed in a 2010 NAMI publication about adolescent depression, which states: "A family history of mood disorders and stressful life events in those who are genetically vulnerable to the condition can lead to the development of depression."[26] The authors go on to explain that some teens develop depression due to chemical imbalances in the brain that are triggered by traumatic occurrences such as grief over a loss, physical and/or sexual abuse, or humiliation or failure. These are considered risk factors, however, rather than definitive causes, and they can affect people in different ways. For instance, a relationship breakup may cause one teen to feel upset for a few days, whereas another teen with biological risk might develop depression.

Family Ties

The scientific theory that multiple factors work together to cause depression has resulted in extensive research. In an effort to understand how these interactions occur, scientists have become particularly interested in genetic risk factors, since depression has been shown to run in families. Numerous studies have revealed that if a first-degree relative (such as a parent) suffers from depression, this markedly increases an individual's risk of also developing it. In a June 2010 article in the American Psychological Association's journal *Focus*, psychiatrist John M. Hettema refers to five separate studies that compared the prevalence of depression among relatives of those who had the illness with the families of healthy study participants. According to Hettema, these studies provide overwhelming evidence that depression is hereditary. They reveal that the risk among individuals who were related to someone with depression was nearly three times higher than for those who did not have a family history of the illness.

Studies with adopted children have strengthened scientists' belief that depression has a genetic component. One study, which was published in September 2008, involved 692 adolescents who had been adopted and 416 who had not. The researchers found that the participants in both groups had a

Numerous studies have shown that if a parent suffers from depression, his or her child will also have an increased risk for the disorder.

significantly higher risk for depression if their biological mothers suffered from the illness. Because this risk pertained to the nonadopted youth as well as those who were adopted, the study suggests that genetics may play a more prominent role in depression than environment.

Because of the strong evidence that depression has genetic ties, scientists have begun trying to identify specific genes that are linked to the illness. Research has shown that the human body contains nearly twenty-five thousand genes, and pinpointing a particular gene (or genes) associated with depression or any other illness is a daunting task. Medical and science journalist Michael Waldholz writes: "Indeed, identifying the precise genes at work in depression has become one of the most sought after scientific prizes being pursued by genome researchers, partly because of how widespread depression is."[27] Through their research, scientists have identified certain genes that make some people more prone to depression than others, and they continue to study those genes. According to the NIMH, though, it is probable that no one gene is solely responsible for depression; rather, the illness likely results from the influence of several genes acting together along with other triggers.

Altered Brain Chemistry

One gene that has been implicated in the development of depression is known as SERT, which helps control how the body uses serotonin. Serotonin is one of several chemicals known as neurotransmitters, whose function is to help relay signals that allow brain cells (called neurons) to communicate with each other. Serotonin influences numerous body functions, including temperature regulation, mood, sleep, appetite, memory, and learning. Some scientists believe that the sleep problems, irritability, and other symptoms associated with depression could be caused by imbalances in serotonin. This could possibly explain why certain teens develop SAD. According to the Mayo Clinic, diminished sunlight during the winter months causes the brain to produce less serotonin, which could trigger the onset of depression.

Researchers are still not certain what a defective SERT gene means for people with depression, but they do know that it plays a crucial role in serotonin regulation. A November 2011 *Scientific American* article explains: "The SERT transports serotonin, after it is released, back into the releasing cells for recycling or breakdown, and so messing with its function can really change how serotonin is being controlled in the brain."[28] Learning more about the effects of a defective SERT gene and how it functions in individuals with depression could help clear up some of the illness's mysteries.

Another neurotransmitter that has been linked to depression is gamma-aminobutyric acid, more commonly known as GABA.

A polarized light micrograph of crystals of the neurotransmitter GABA is seen here. GABA's most important function is to inhibit excessive nerve transmission in the brain, thus calming nerve activity.

This chemical plays an essential role in brain functions such as moods, thoughts, and actions. According to Andrea Levinson of Canada's Centre for Addiction and Medical Health, one of GABA's most important functions is to inhibit excessive nerve transmission in the brain, which means it is essential for calming nervous activity. Says Levinson: "It's a little like driving a car. You need the accelerator, but at every stage you need the brakes to work. Some of our neurotransmitters apply the spark and the gas to the engine, and GABA supplies the brakes."[29] Levinson theorizes that if GABA levels are too low in someone with depression, this could be responsible for the excessive negative thinking that is characteristic of the disorder.

In March 2010 Levinson and her colleagues announced the results of a study that examined the link between depression and altered levels of GABA in the brain. To perform this study, the researchers used a type of advanced technology known as transcranial magnetic stimulation (TMS), which uses magnetic fields to stimulate neurons. Using TMS, the team measured how GABA reacted in the brains of people with major depression, as well as in the brains of twenty-five healthy study participants (known as the control group). The study revealed that GABA function was not working properly in the depressed participants but was performing normally in those who did not have depression.

GABA's connection with depression in teenagers was the focus of a study published in October 2011 by researchers from the New York University School of Medicine. The study involved forty-one teens, including twenty who had depression and twenty-one who did not. Half of the depressed teens also suffered from a condition called anhedonia, which is common among young people with depression and involves the inability to experience pleasure. Using a type of specialized magnetic resonance imaging (MRI) to measure GABA levels in the brain, the researchers found that the depressed teens had significantly lower GABA levels than those in the control group. The study also found that the teens with the lowest GABA levels were those who had the most severe anhedonia symptoms. In a review of the study, the NIMH writes: "The findings support a role for GABA in anhedonia and depression among

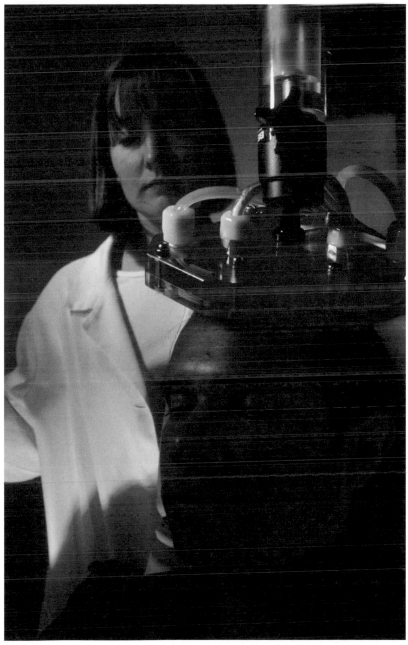

A doctor uses a high-powered magnet to stimulate brain activity in an experimental treatment for depression. The treatment allows researchers to measure how GABA reacts in the brains of people with major depression.

teens. . . . Advances in imaging techniques and technology may help to identify differing roles for other neurotransmitters associated with depression."[30]

The Role of Hormones

Other chemicals in the body, such as hormones, are also believed to be associated with depression. The function of hormones is to carry messages from organs to cells in order to coordinate various bodily functions and maintain the body's natural balance. In response to signals from the brain, hormones are released by endocrine glands, which include the thyroid, adrenals (glands atop to the kidneys), pituitary, pancreas, and reproductive gland, among others. At the start of puberty, which is a time of immense hormonal changes, the brain signals the pituitary gland to release sex hormones into the bloodstream. In boys these hormones alert the testes to begin producing testosterone and sperm, whereas in girls the hormones stimulate the ovaries to produce a hormone known as estrogen. According to the National Institutes of Health, the hormonal changes that take place during puberty likely influence the development of depression in teens. Exactly how and why this occurs, however, is not clear.

Another hormone that has been of interest to scientists studying depression is cortisol, which the body produces in response to stress, anger, or fear. When faced with a dangerous or stressful situation, cortisol levels in the body are naturally elevated—but when there is too much of the hormone in the bloodstream, it can lead to health problems. Kate Harkness, a Canadian psychologist who has extensively studied stress and trauma, explains: "Over time cortisol levels can build up and increase a person's risk for more severe endocrine impairment and more severe depression."[31] According to Harkness, the risk of depression is elevated because excess cortisol kills cells in areas of the brain that control memory and emotion regulation.

Harkness is part of a research team that has analyzed the effects of excessive cortisol in the brains of teenagers. One study, which was published in February 2011, examined the connection between stress hormones and depression in young people who had a history of child abuse. The study involved seventy-one youth aged twelve to twenty-one, including some who suffered from depression and others who did not. The participants were given psychological tests that put them under stress, such as giving a speech or solving difficult math problems. Saliva samples were taken at various intervals during the testing so the researchers could measure changes in each participant's cortisol levels. At the conclusion of the study, the team found that the depressed teens with a history of abuse produced higher and more prolonged levels of cortisol in response to the test challenges compared with participants without a history of abuse. This finding suggests that cortisol levels in the child abuse victims were elevated when they were young, which later affected areas of the brain responsible for memory and regulation of emotions.

Stress, Trauma, and Grief

Harkness's study is not the first to examine the connection between child maltreatment and depression in teens. Prior research has also shown that physical, sexual, and emotional abuse, as well as neglect, at a young age can change brain chemistry and increase a child's risk of developing illnesses such as depression later in life. The same is true of many types of trauma that can affect young children, such as the death of a parent or other significant person, or extreme turmoil in the family. The American Academy of Child & Adolescent Psychiatry writes: "[Children] may live in families where they regularly witness or are victims of parental aggression, rejection or scapegoating, strict and punitive treatment, and parents abusing each other. Such family pressures may contribute to the development of depressed mood disturbance in a teenager."[32]

Stressful life events, however, can also affect teens who were not abused as children and whose family lives were not filled with turmoil. Difficulties during adolescence such as dysfunctional relationships or loss (like breaking up with a boyfriend or girlfriend), moving to a new neighborhood, changing schools, or being bullied have all been shown to contribute to depression in teens, especially those who are already biologically vulnerable.

The "Facebook Depression" Theory

Social media sites are extremely popular with people all over the world. One example is Facebook, which reached 901 million active users in April 2012 and continues to grow in popularity every day. According to a report by the American Academy of Pediatrics, using social media sites is among the most common activities of teenagers and is one that provides them with a portal for entertainment and communication—and that possibly contributes to the development of depression. The report states:

Researchers have proposed a new phenomenon called "Facebook depression," defined as depression that develops when preteens and teens spend a great deal of time on social media sites, such as Facebook, and then begin to exhibit classic symptoms of depression. Acceptance by and contact with peers is an important element of adolescent life. The intensity of the online world is thought to be a factor that may trigger depression in some adolescents. As with offline depression, preadolescents and adolescents who suffer from Facebook depression are at risk for social isolation and sometimes turn to risky Internet sites and blogs for "help" that may promote substance abuse, unsafe sexual practices, or aggressive or self-destructive behaviors.

Gwenn Schurgin O'Keeffe, Kathleen Clarke-Pearson, and the Council on Communications and Media. "Clinical Report—the Impact of Social Media on Children, Adolescents, and Families." *Pediatrics*, March 28, 2011. http://pediatrics.aappublications.org /content/early/2011/03/28/peds.2011-0054.full.pdf.

Some researchers suggest that teens can develop "Facebook depression" from spending too much time on social networking sites.

Lisa Furst, who is with the Mental Health Association of New York City, explains: "While most youth will experience painful or difficult feelings during periods of stress and develop adequate coping mechanisms to help them adjust to the stressful situation, some youth may experience longer-lasting reactions, including depression."[33]

For Matt Gallagher, who began to show signs of depression when he was sixteen years old, the stressful situation was his parents' divorce. He was devastated at the thought of losing his dad and felt abandoned by him. Also, since Gallagher was the oldest of four children, he felt a great deal of pressure to help his mother with his siblings. He felt the stress piling up until it seemed overwhelming, and then his personality radically changed. Previously happy, outgoing, and popular in school, Gallagher began withdrawing from his friends and sleeping much more than usual. When he began displaying uncharacteristically angry outbursts, his mother knew something was very wrong and took him to a doctor, who diagnosed depression. "I knew we were struggling," she says. "But I didn't realize to what point."[34]

Too Much Pressure?

Many teens say that the pressure they face can be overwhelming. According to some mental health professionals, today's teens are under such high pressure to excel that they are more prone to depression than young people were in past generations. This is the perspective of Matthew Soulier, a psychiatrist with the University of California–Davis, who explains: "I think there's a drive to be 'the best' in a way there wasn't before." Soulier adds that it is no longer enough for young people merely to participate in a choir, be part of a sports team, or just be average kids: "[These days] you have to have a coach. You have to excel, build the perfect resume, get into the right college. The expectations are so big."[35]

A study that was released in January 2010 revealed that young people today endure far more stress than teens of their parents' and grandparents' generations. It was conducted by researchers from five universities, including San Diego State

University, who analyzed nearly eighty thousand responses to a psychological questionnaire. Known as the Minnesota Multiphasic Personality Inventory, the test has been completed by high school and college students in the United States since the 1930s. Based on an analysis of student responses, the researchers concluded that the number of young people with depression was six times higher in 2007 than it was in 1938. The reasons for this are not known, although lead researcher Jean Twenge says the findings clearly indicate that there is a growing depression problem among teenagers. She acknowledges, though, that additional research is needed to fully understand why. "It's another piece of the puzzle,"[36] says Twenge.

The study was one of the most comprehensive analyses of teen depression that has ever been done, but it was not the first indication that the illness has grown among adolescents. Prior research has also shown that teen depression is more common today than it was in the past. Although the reasons for this are not well understood, mental health experts have several theories. One possible explanation is that today, more than ever before, young people are under intense pressure because of society's emphasis on wealth, personal appearance, and social status. Many experts say that being constantly exposed to such unattainable expectations can lead to a sense of failure and deep disappointment for teens. Mental Health America writes that because of these unrealistic expectations, "many young people feel that life is not fair or that things 'never go their way.' They feel 'stressed out' and confused. To make matters worse, teens are bombarded by conflicting messages from parents, friends and society. Today's teens see more of what life has to offer—both good and bad—on television, at school, in magazines and on the Internet."[37]

Emily Fagan is convinced that the enormous pressure she put on herself to be the best at everything played a major role in her depression. As a sophomore in high school she was not only an honors student, but also a student ambassador and a member of the principal's advisory committee. She played oboe and English horn in four school bands and a youth symphony orchestra, was in the choir, and was active in the drama

Psychologist James N. Butcher holds a copy of the Minnesota Multiphasic Personality Inventory. The test, first created in the 1930s, showed in a study released in 2010 that young people today suffer from depression at a rate six times higher than that of youth in the 1930s.

club. On top of all these activities, Emily also took piano, oboe, and voice lessons, played music at church on Sundays, and was involved with softball and theater during the summer. She explains: "I have always had a Type-A personality, striving for perfection, trying to do everything. I was addicted to perfection."[38] After experiencing a breakdown in 2009, Emily was hospitalized and spent a month in a residential treatment center.

Risky Weed

Health officials have long been concerned about the potential harm of marijuana on adolescents, largely because the drug is known to affect brain function. In October 2011 a team of Dutch researchers announced the findings of a five-year study that revealed another hazard of smoking marijuana—an increased risk of developing depression. The study involved over eight hundred teenagers from the Netherlands, where marijuana is legal for adults and available in coffee shops. Nearly 30 percent of the sixteen-year-old participants indicated that they had smoked marijuana at least once, and 12 percent said they had used it recently.

At the conclusion of the study, the researchers determined that teens can vastly increase their risk of developing depression if they smoke marijuana. The authors write:

Some people might think that young people with a disposition for depression would start smoking cannabis as a form of self-medication and that the presence of depressive symptoms is therefore the cause of cannabis use. However, in the longer term that is definitely not the case. Although the immediate effect of cannabis may be pleasant and cause a feeling of euphoria, in the longer term we observe that cannabis use leads to an increase in depressive symptoms in young people [who are genetically vulnerable].

Quoted in David McCracken. "Dutch Study Shows Cannabis Tied to Risk of Depression in Youth." Psych Central, October 17, 2011. http://psychcentral.com/news/2011/10/17/dutch-study-shows-cannabis-tied-to-risk-of-depression-in-youth/30370.html.

Dutch researchers have concluded that teens who smoke marijuana increase their risk of developing depression.

Finally, she faced the fact that all the pressure she put on herself was too overwhelming and a major factor in her illness.

Lives "Turned Upside Down"

Teens who live with chronic illness are very familiar with the concept of feeling overwhelmed, and research has shown that chronically ill teens have a markedly higher risk of developing depression than healthy teens. An estimated 8 percent of healthy youth aged twelve to seventeen are affected by depression. According to New York psychologist Jean-Marie Bruzzese, about 15 percent of teens with asthma suffer from depression, as do 25 percent of those with inflammatory bowel disease, in which the intestines are chronically inflamed. Bruzzese explains: "When children have a chronic disease their lives can be turned upside down. . . . It is easy to understand why depression often goes hand in hand with a chronic disease."[39]

One reason depression is so common among chronically ill teenagers is that their disease can cause tremendous changes in their lifestyles and, depending on the seriousness of the illness, can restrict their independence. They may find that they can no longer pursue activities they once enjoyed, which can damage their self-worth and confidence and diminish their hopes for the future. A September 2009 article on WebMD explains: "It is not surprising then, that people with chronic illness often experience a certain amount of despair and sadness " The article goes on to say that the depression caused by chronic illness often aggravates the condition and makes it worse, such as intensifying pain and fatigue. "The combination of chronic illness and depression also can cause people to isolate themselves, which is likely to [worsen] the depression."[40]

One chronic illness that has a strong connection with depression is epilepsy, which is characterized by recurrent seizures (or convulsions) caused by erratic brain activity. A 2006 study by British researchers found that among teenagers with epilepsy, up to 60 percent also suffered from depression or another psychiatric illness. The combination of disorders can be a tremendous burden. Sigita Plioplys, a pediatric psychiatrist in the Department of Child and Adolescent Psychiatry

This woman suffers from epilepsy, which has been shown to be accompanied by depression in 60 percent of epileptic young people.

at Children's Memorial Hospital in Chicago, explains: "Kids with epilepsy are sort of hit twice. There's an enormous stigma associated with epilepsy, and they may feel ashamed or burdened by having epilepsy. And mental disorders also have a profound stigma attached to them. Many kids will tend to minimize their depressive symptoms until they can't function anymore."[41]

Similar findings about the connection between epilepsy and depression resulted from a more recent study that was conducted by researchers from Norway. At the conclusion of their research, which was published in 2011, the team determined that epilepsy was a significant risk factor for depression—stronger than poverty, living with a single parent, or having any other type of chronic disease.

A Complex, Mysterious Illness

Scientists have studied depression for decades, and they have gained an immense amount of knowledge about the illness—but they cannot say, with any certainty, what causes it. Research has, however, revealed a number of likely factors such as genetics, brain chemistry, and environmental triggers like trauma, grief, and stress. Although none of these factors have been definitively proved to cause depression single-handedly, research strongly suggests that the factors work together in complex ways in the development of the illness. As studies continue in the future, scientists will expand their knowledge of depression, which may bring them closer to solving the mystery of how and why it develops.

CHAPTER THREE

Diagnosis and Treatment

As distressing as depression can be for teens who suffer from it, they can take comfort in knowing that it is among the most treatable of all mental illnesses. According to the NIMH, the earlier treatment begins, the more effective it can be, which means that young people who are treated have an excellent chance of recovering. Treatments for depression vary from person to person, because they are based on someone's individual symptoms and unique needs. A young woman named Sarah, who overcame major depression after a four-year battle that began when she was fifteen years old, explains: "In order to properly treat depression there are different combinations of treatment one must try. If you're lucky enough to find that your first treatment option works, that's great! But I had to go through a couple different options in order to find the best fit. Treatment is really like finding an awesome fitting shirt. You have to try a lot on to find the perfect one!"[42]

A Crucial First Step

Before Sarah was diagnosed and treated for depression, she had to do something that was far from easy—admit to herself that the emotional pain, confusion, and constant irritation she was experiencing was much more than normal teenage moodiness.

Unfortunately, many teenagers never do that. Either they convince themselves that they are just going through a phase (as Sarah did at first), or they are too ashamed or afraid to reach out for help. According to an April 2011 report by the Substance Abuse and Mental Health Services Administration

A 2011 report by the Substance Abuse and Mental Health Services Administration stated that nearly two-thirds of adolescents who suffered from major depression in 2009 were not treated for it.

(SAMHSA), nearly two-thirds of adolescents who suffered from major depression in 2009 were not treated. Although the exact reasons are unknown, experts say this is likely because teens try to hide their symptoms rather than tell anyone what they are going through. The SAMHSA report states: "These findings highlight the need to raise awareness of the signs of adolescent depression, to increase screening for adolescent depression in multiple health care settings, and to more widely disseminate information on the availability of treatment and treatment options."[43]

Therese J. Borchard, who is associate editor of the Psych Central website and the author of the book *Beyond Blue: Surviving Depression & Anxiety and Making the Most of Bad Genes*, began to experience signs of depression when she was a teenager. She says that the smartest thing she ever did was open up about her problem to a kind teacher whom she trusted and respected. This, says Borchard, was the first step toward a path of recovery that changed her life. She writes: "Sometimes it's easier to approach someone outside your family because a parent wants to believe everything is fine and might not be able to face real problems. I urge you to get the help you need by asking an adult that you know won't judge you but will find the appropriate resources."[44]

Arriving at a Diagnosis

When depressed teens seek professional help, most start by visiting their family physician. Although there is no specific medical or diagnostic test that can detect depression, qualified health-care professionals have procedures that can help determine whether a teen is truly depressed or suffering from another kind of problem. The first step is usually a complete physical examination, including a series of laboratory tests. These tests can detect possible medical conditions such as viruses, a thyroid problem, or anemia, a disorder in which the blood does not contain enough healthy red blood cells to carry oxygen to tissues. It is important to test for these conditions because each can cause symptoms that resemble depression. Doctors also perform blood tests to determine whether the

Once medical conditions and substance abuse have been ruled out as a cause of a depressed patient's symptoms, a psychologist or psychiatrist will complete a psychological evaluation.

teen has been using drugs or alcohol, as these substances can also cause depressive symptoms.

Once all possible medical conditions and substance abuse have been ruled out, the doctor (or mental health practitioner) performs a psychological evaluation. This involves talking to the teen about thoughts, feelings, and behaviors, to determine what symptoms he or she has exhibited, how severe those

Healing with Light

Scientists believe that a type of depression known as seasonal affective disorder (SAD) is closely connected with diminished sunlight during the cloudy, dreary winter months. This theory is strengthened by the fact that the disorder is seldom found in countries within 30 degrees of the equator, where the sun shines year-round. So, one of the main treatments for teens with SAD is to increase their exposure to light through what is known as bright light therapy. This involves having the patient sit under artificial light for a set period of time each day, as a March 2010 WebMD article explains:

> With light therapy for SAD, you sit about 2 feet from a bright light (about 20 times brighter than normal room lighting). You start with one 10-minute to 15-minute session per day. The time is then increased to 30 minutes–45 minutes a day, depending on your response. . . . If the SAD symptoms don't stop, your doctor may increase the light therapy sessions to twice daily. Those who respond to light therapy are encouraged to continue until they can be out in the sunshine again in springtime.

The article goes on to state that some researchers link SAD to the natural hormone melatonin, which causes drowsiness. Because light has been shown to modify the amount of melatonin in the human nervous system, as well as boost serotonin in the brain, light therapy has an antidepressant effect.

WebMD. "Seasonal Depression (Seasonal Affective Disorder)," March 1, 2010. www.webmd.com/depression/guide/seasonal-affective-disorder.

Depression due to seasonal affective disorder is treated with light, or phototherapy.

symptoms are, and whether the teen has had suicidal thoughts or is in any immediate danger of self-harm. Another purpose of the evaluation is to distinguish depression from a normal sense of sadness or grief. In most cases parents and other family members will be interviewed and asked to describe changes in the teen's behavior such as unusual moodiness and/or irritability, changes in sleep and appetite, declining grades, loss of interest in favorite activities, and other depressive symptoms as defined in the DSM-IV. The NAMI explains the importance of a comprehensive medical and psychological evaluation before a diagnosis is made, to ensure an individualized treatment plan: "It is important to have a real understanding of the stresses and strengths a youth brings to the equation. It is also essential to have the youth be a part of the emerging plan. There is no 'one size fits all'— mental health interventions need to be tailored to the individual."[45]

Working Through the Pain

Although treatment plans are developed on an individual basis, most involve one or more types of psychotherapy, which involves counseling sessions with a trained mental health professional. Two psychotherapy methods that have proved to be effective for teens with depression are interpersonal therapy and cognitive behavioral therapy (CBT). With the former, the therapist provides support and empathy in a safe environment where the teen feels free to talk openly and honestly about his or her problems. In the course of these conversations, the therapist encourages the teen to open up about what may have precipitated the depression. For instance, if the teen has endured family turmoil, problems in school, or the death of a loved one or other traumatic event, he or she can work through unresolved feelings and eventually accept the reality of the situation, as painful as it may be. The American Academy of Child & Adolescent Psychiatry explains: "Therapy helps the adolescent deal with these feelings rather than act them out. If a teenager's self-esteem seems particularly low, therapy may work to improve confidence and competence through skills training."[46]

CBT also involves talking with a therapist, but its focus is on modifying behavior; specifically, changing unhealthy patterns of thinking. In CBT sessions teens learn how to think more realistically rather than viewing themselves, the world, the future, and even life itself in a negative way. The Dartmouth Medical School calls this "black or white" thinking, as the group explains: "This is when a person thinks that things are only 'good' if they are perfect. If something isn't perfect, they think [it] is completely 'bad' and a complete failure. CBT will teach a 'black or white' thinker to recognize that even if something isn't perfect it can still be pretty good or good enough."[47]

Another example of unhealthy thinking addressed in CBT sessions is when a depressed teen "rejects the positive." With this kind of thought process, the teen rejects anything good that happens, as though it does not count. The therapist will ask questions that prompt the teen to see that his or her perceptions and/or interpretations may be false, which leads to negative views. The Dartmouth group writes: "CBT will teach someone who thinks like this to enjoy good feelings when they have them."[48]

To illustrate a depressed teenager's negative thinking, clinical psychologist Marc Skelton uses the scenario of a boy who asks a girl out on a date and is rejected. Says Skelton: "He gets depressed because he interprets the rejection as 'I'm not worthy. I am just a screw-up.' As the therapist, you try to get him to see that it's just one person saying no for any number of reasons and not because he's a bad person."[49] By participating in CBT the boy learns that being turned down for one date does not mean he is unworthy or a "screw-up," and he is taught to replace such negative, self-defeating perceptions with more realistic, positive thoughts. The therapist may accomplish this by assigning "homework" for him to work on between sessions. For example, the teen may be assigned to ask three or four different girls to do something with him in order to apply what he and the therapist have talked about in their sessions.

Group and Family Therapy

Two other types of therapy that are often recommended for teens with depression are group therapy and counseling that involves the whole family. Group therapy is a form of psychotherapy in which multiple patients participate in sessions led by one or more therapists. It uses the collective power of group interaction and education to help depressed patients better understand their illness, while at the same time reinforcing that they are not alone in their struggles. The group approach was extremely helpful for Olivia Thompson when she was being treated for depression, as she explains: "You're sitting in a circle and talking with everyone. I didn't know how many people feel just like me."[50] Another important benefit of group therapy is that by talking to others about what they are going through, teens can often develop and/or improve social skills, which can help strengthen their self-esteem.

Family therapy can also be beneficial for depressed teens because it helps the whole family interact and learn to communicate in positive, constructive ways. The thinking behind this type of therapy is that when the family functions better, the depressed teen will also be able to function better. Sessions address problems that have potentially contributed to the

An important benefit of group therapy is the development or improvement of teens' social skills, which helps strengthen their self-esteem.

teen's illness or made it worse, such as family conflict, lack of clear boundaries, rules that are overly rigid or inconsistent, and dysfunctional parent-child relationships. Psychiatrists Pamela Broderick and Christina Weston explain: "Family therapy shifts the focus of the psychiatrist's attention away from the child and onto the family as both the source of [the problem] and the target for treatment. It is clear that a child's mental health stems both from genetic factors and from family dynamics. Although a child's genetics cannot, at this time, be modified, the family dynamics are at our disposal."[51]

In a January 2009 paper published in the medical journal *Innovations in Clinical Neuroscience*, Broderick and Weston discuss the use of family therapy in helping a fifteen-year-old boy overcome depression. The boy, whom they refer to as "J," had grown increasingly depressed over a period of several months. He was struggling in school, felt like he did not fit in with his classmates, and suffered from near-constant sadness, decreased energy, and problems sleeping. Turmoil in his family was contributing to his depressed feelings, which is why family therapy was recommended. Broderick and Weston describe one session in which J and his stepfather were encouraged to talk to each other about an incident when the boy's stepfather caught him smoking in his bedroom.

> Psychiatrist: J, can you tell me what you remember about the time you were caught smoking?
>
> J: I was in my room and I thought my parents were still at work when my dad bursts open my door and [starts] yelling. I was afraid he was going to hit me he looked so mad.
>
> Psychiatrist: Can you look at your dad and tell that story again to him?
>
> J: I guess. . . . Dad, I was really scared by you when you were yelling. I know I did something wrong but. . . .
>
> Stepfather: (Looking at psychiatrist) I didn't mean to scare him.

Psychiatrist: Dad, can you say that to J.

Stepfather: I didn't mean to scare you, but I know you are really a good kid at heart and it hurts me to see you making stupid decisions.[52]

By leading this kind of interactive discussion, the therapist is able to help family members recognize how communication breakdowns occur and to offer solutions to help resolve them if they do happen. Family members also learn the importance of listening and being sensitive to each other's points of view.

Combination Treatment

As valuable as psychotherapy can be for depressed teens, numerous mental health professionals believe that the most successful treatment plans include both therapy and medication with drugs known as antidepressants. The American Academy of Child & Adolescent Psychiatry explains: "In milder forms of depression, it is reasonable to start with a psychotherapy, but treatment with a medication and psychotherapy should be considered for moderate to severe forms of major depression."[53] The benefits of combination treatment were revealed during a study that was published by the NIMH in 2004. Known as the Treatment for Adolescents with Depression Study (TADS), it examined three different treatment plans for teens with moderate to severe depression. One group was given the antidepressant medication fluoxetine (Prozac), another group underwent CBT, and the third group was treated with a combination of CBT and antidepressants. After twelve weeks, 71 percent of the teens involved in the combination treatment improved significantly, compared with 61 percent who only took medication and 43 percent who were only assigned CBT.

A more recent TADS study was published in the October 2009 issue of the *American Journal of Psychiatry* and yielded even more impressive findings. As with the earlier study, participants were assigned to one of three treatment groups. By the end of the thirty-six-week trial, 82 percent of the teens who were treated with CBT and antidepressants had improved, and 59 percent had reached full remission, not experiencing any

depressive symptoms. During the follow-up year, most participants maintained their improvements, and the remission rate
climbed to 68 percent. The NIMH writes: "The results suggest
that combination treatment is the safest and most effective
treatment overall for adolescents with depression."[54]

Despite such positive findings, however, the use of antidepressants with teenagers is somewhat controversial, as several studies have shown that these medications can increase
suicidal thoughts in young patients. Because of that, the U.S.
Food and Drug Administration issued a "black box" warning
(the strongest safety warning the agency issues) about antidepressant use among youth under the age of eighteen. Although
the American Academy of Child & Adolescent Psychiatry acknowledges that the drugs have been associated with a minor
increase in suicidal thoughts among teenagers, the group emphasizes that antidepressant use has not been definitively
linked to an increase in teen suicide. Thus, the academy remains convinced that for moderate to severe depression, "the
potential benefits from medication treatment seem to outweigh the potential risks."[55]

Benefits of a Healthy Lifestyle

As successful as psychotherapy and antidepressant medication has proved to be in treating depressed teens, adding a
healthy diet and exercise to the equation can improve their
lives even more. Scientists have long been aware that eating
certain foods and avoiding others can improve health and well-
being, and many are convinced that eating right can also help
someone overcome depression. Borchard explains: "Just as
certain foods and drinks can lead to depression—processed
white flour, sweets, caffeine, sodas—others actually lift your
mood." According to Borchard, some of the most valuable
foods are those that contain the omega-3 fatty acids, which are
found in salmon and other oily fish, flaxseeds, walnuts, and
eggs. Also beneficial are foods that are rich in vitamin B_{12} and
folate, a B vitamin that is essential for cell growth and repro-
duction. Borchard writes: "Some scientists believe that these
vitamins create serotonin, which normalizes mood. Vitamin D

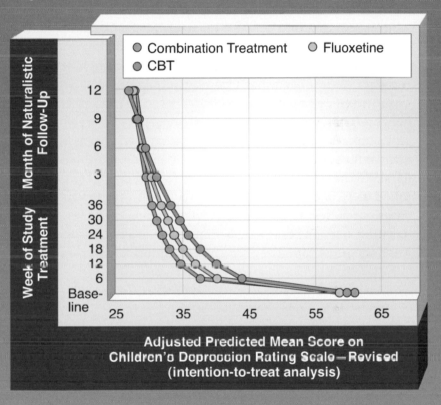

NIMH's Treatment for Adolescents with Depression Study (TADS)

Depression scores from baseline to end of naturalistic follow-up for 327 adolescents with major depressive disorder treated with fluoxetine, cognitive behavioral therapy (CBT), or a combination.

○ Combination Treatment   ○ Fluoxetine
○ CBT

Month of Naturalistic Follow-Up

12
9
6
3

Week of Study Treatment

36
30
24
18
12
6
Base-line

25   35   45   55   65

Adjusted Predicted Mean Score on Children's Depression Rating Scale—Revised (intention-to-treat analysis)

Taken from: NIMH: Treatment for Adolescents with Depression Study, 2009.
ajp.psychiatryonline.org/article.aspx?volume=166&page=1141&journalID=13.

also increases serotonin and can be especially helpful with Seasonal Affective Disorder (SAD). Milk and soy milk are full of Vitamin D as are egg yolks and fish with bones."[56]

Examining the benefits of a healthy diet for teens with depression was the focus of a 2011 study by researchers from Australia. The study involved over two thousand adolescents aged eleven to eighteen who were participants in a lifestyle

Stimulating the Brain

Although depression can be successfully treated with a combination of psychotherapy and antidepressant medications, sometimes teens do not respond to these treatments. In that case physicians might recommend a relatively new procedure known as transcranial magnetic stimulation (TMS), which uses magnetic fields to alter brain activity. During a treatment session, which is done on an outpatient basis, an electromagnetic coil is placed against the scalp near the forehead. This coil produces an electrical current in the brain to stimulate neurons that are involved in mood control and depression. No anesthesia is necessary, the patient feels no pain, and side effects (if any) are mild. According to the Mayo Clinic, how TMS helps relieve depression is not completely understood, as the group writes: "It's thought that magnetic pulses stimulate nerve cells in the region of your brain involved in mood control. This stimulation appears to alter how this part of the brain is working, which in turn seems to ease depression symptoms and improve mood."

Mayo Clinic. "Transcranial Magnetic Stimulation: Why It's Done," May 25, 2011. www.mayoclinic.com/health/transcranial-magnetic-stimulation/MY00185/DSEC TION=why-its-done.

A patient is treated with transcranial magnetic stimulation to treat depression.

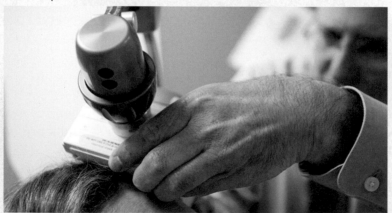

program called It's Your Move. Each student completed a survey with questions about factors such as nutrition, mental health, and physical activity, as well as perceptions of home and school environments. The questions, which were specific to diet, covered healthy eating (plenty of fruits and vegetables and general avoidance of processed foods such as chips, fried foods, and sweets) versus unhealthy eating (diets high in snack and processed foods). At the conclusion of the study, the researchers determined that the teens with the healthiest diets had better overall mental health than those whose diets were unhealthy. The study authors write: "We found individuals with better quality diets were less likely to be depressed, whereas a higher intake of processed and unhealthy foods was associated with increased anxiety."[57]

A healthy lifestyle includes not only a nutritious diet but exercise, which has also been connected with lower incidence of depression among teens. Research suggests that exercise improves people's moods because it alters brain chemistry by regulating serotonin in much the same way that antidepressants do. This was a major finding of an analysis that involved statistically summarizing eighty studies of exercise and depression. Although the analysis was conducted in 1990, it is still considered one of the most important studies ever done on exercise and depression. It revealed that exercise served as a beneficial antidepressant both immediately and over the long term, that it decreased depression among all groups surveyed, and that the greater the length of the exercise program, the more significant the decrease in depression. According to the APA, "Evidence of the antidepressant benefits of exercise is being used by psychotherapists and other health practitioners who are increasingly recommending exercise to their patients as part of a treatment program."[58]

One psychologist who strongly recommends an exercise regimen for people with depression is Jasper Smiths. He says that his depressed patients who have started exercising have noticed improvements in how they feel almost immediately. For those who are not motivated to exercise, he gives them a reason why they should *become* motivated: a marked decrease

Research suggests that exercise improves people's moods because it alters brain chemistry by regulating serotonin in much the same way antidepressants do.

in stress and improvements in their mood. He explains: "You feel crappy, so you get on the treadmill, and you look back and you say, 'Wow, I feel much better.'"[59]

Plentiful Options, Positive Outlook

Depression is a difficult, emotionally painful illness, but treatment can significantly improve the quality of life for teens who suffer from it. A wide variety of treatment options are available for depressed teens, including individual, family, and group therapy; cognitive behavioral therapy; and antidepressant medications, all of which have been proved to treat depression successfully. When teens maintain healthy lifestyles, including eating nutritious foods and exercising regularly, they improve their chances of overcoming depression even more. According to Mental Health America, depressed teens often have a tough time believing that life can get better—but it can, as the group writes: "Professional treatment can have a dramatic impact on their lives. It can put them back on track and bring them hope for the future."[60]

CHAPTER FOUR

Living with Depression

Teens can have a very hard time coping with the effects of depression. Many suffer from a sense of guilt, as though they are somehow at fault for having an illness. Also typical for depressed teens is to feel like everyone is against them—their parents scold them for being grouchy all the time, and their friends no longer find them fun to be around. This can take a heavy toll on young people who are struggling with depression, making them feel sad and hopeless. As hard as it may be when they find themselves sinking into despair, teens are encouraged to fight back rather than give in to their illness. Mental health specialists Melinda Smith, Robert Segal, and Jeanne Segal write: "Depression drains your energy, hope, and drive, making it difficult to do what you need to feel better. But while overcoming depression isn't quick or easy, it's far from impossible."[61] They acknowledge that it takes time for depressed teens to feel better. But a happier life is within reach if they make positive choices for themselves while also drawing on the support of others.

Embracing Support

Accepting the support of family and friends is an important first step in the fight against depression, but reaching out may be the last thing depressed teens want to do. Instead, they tend to withdraw and isolate themselves from others. They may be embarrassed and ashamed of their symptoms, frustrated over what is happening to them, or overwhelmed by all that they are facing. One teen who can relate to these feelings is Kirk Zajac, who says his bout with depression was like "being in a black hole." Zajac was fourteen when he suddenly began to feel listless and sleepy much of the time, and he began to withdraw from everyone. He explains: "I just put on my happy face for the rest of the world and went out there, did what I had to do and went home and literally sat and did nothing and [steeped] in my depression."[62]

Even though teens may find it distressing to reach out to others and admit they need help, doing so is an essential part

Depression drains one's energy, hope, and drive, making it difficult to do what one needs to do to feel better.

Coping Strategies

Stress is a fact of life for many teenagers who suffer from depression, and learning stress-management skills can help them immensely. The American Academy of Child & Adolescent Psychiatry offers these behaviors and techniques to help teens decrease stress:

- Exercise and eat regular, healthy meals.

- Avoid excess caffeine intake, which can increase feelings of anxiety and agitation.

- Avoid illegal drugs, alcohol, and tobacco.

- Learn relaxation exercises such as abdominal breathing and muscle relaxation techniques.

- Develop assertiveness training skills. State feelings politely and firmly, rather than in overly aggressive or passive ways: ("I feel angry when you yell at me." "Please stop yelling.")

- Rehearse and practice situations that cause stress. One example is taking a speech class if talking in front of a class makes you anxious.

- Learn practical coping skills, such as breaking large tasks into smaller, more attainable tasks.

- Learn to feel good about doing a competent or "good enough" job rather than demanding perfection from yourself and others.

- Take a break from stressful situations. Activities like listening to music, talking to a friend, drawing, writing, or spending time with a pet can reduce stress.

- Build a network of friends who help you cope in positive ways.

American Academy of Child & Adolescent Psychiatry. "Helping Teenagers with Stress." *Facts for Families*, May 2005.

of coping with depression. In her book *The 10 Best-Ever Depression Management Techniques*, psychologist Margaret Wehrenberg refers to this as a vicious cycle, in which the longer young people remain isolated, the more depressed they are and the more they become convinced that no one really understands or cares about them—as untrue as that may be. As she explains:

> If you are unhappy and find being around others to be a source of irritation, you are probably radiating signals that you are irritable. . . . Although you want to be soothed, you are unlikely to receive that response. Family and friends will pull away if you are crabby enough to be unpleasant to be around. As you have less contact with people who could support you—who could mitigate your mood, offer you some perspective, divert your attention away from yourself—you go deeper into your depression.[63]

If a teen does not reach out to others, friends who notice uncharacteristic changes in personality and behavior should not hesitate to speak up. Carol Glod, who is a child and adolescent mental health specialist, encourages young people to pay attention when a friend's behavior does not seem right and ask questions in a nonconfrontational way. She explains: "It is important to be supportive and to say things like, 'I am very concerned about you. You are saying things that I am really worried about, and we need to tell somebody. Let's talk to your parents, or the guidance department or the school nurse." Glod adds that if the depressed teen does not want anyone else to know what he or she is going through, friends should not abide by that wish—even if it means breaking a confidence and making the person angry. She acknowledges that this is a very hard thing for teenagers to do. "Teens don't want to jeopardize a friendship," says Glod, "but on the other hand, people with depression can end up killing themselves. Or, their depression gets worse and worse and worse, and leads to drug and alcohol problems."[64]

The intervening of a caring friend may have saved the life of a teenage girl named Lynn. Formerly outgoing and cheerful,

Lynn had become so depressed that she was constantly sad, her grades were slipping, and she ate almost nothing. When she became dangerously thin, it was obvious to her friends that she was in trouble, but she would not talk to them about it. The turning point came when Lynn and her best friend, Jamie, got into a screaming match that ended with Lynn telling Jamie everything. Jamie told her own parents, who then told Lynn's parents, and Lynn finally opened up about her problem. "I was at the point where I wanted to die," she says. Today, when Lynn looks back on that frightening time in her life, she cannot help thinking that reaching out to Jamie is what ultimately saved her. She explains: "I was so worried that she'd look at me weird. But, without her, I don't know what would've happened to me."[65]

One Step at a Time

Before Lynn's friend reached out to her, she had become severely withdrawn, which is common among teens who suffer from depression. As difficult as it may be, however, it is important that they put effort into doing things that take their minds off themselves and their misery. Becoming isolated and avoiding activities and hobbies they once enjoyed is not healthy behavior. In an October 2011 article on the mental health site Helpguide.org, Suzanne Barston, Melinda Smith, and Jeanne Segal suggest to depressed individuals: "Push yourself to do things, even when you don't feel like it. You might be surprised at how much better you feel once you're out in the world. Even if your depression doesn't lift immediately, you'll gradually feel more upbeat and energetic as you make time for fun activities."[66]

Mayo Clinic psychiatrist David Mrazek agrees that depression can greatly diminish teens' desire to get up and get moving, as he explains: "You may think, how am I going to find energy or motivation when I feel so poorly?" Although Mrazek suggests that depressed teens become involved in enjoyable activities or hobbies, he encourages them not to take on too much at once. Rather, they should begin with small steps and work up from there. For instance, if a teenage boy was on his school track team before developing depression, he may have lost all enthusiasm for running. Even if he starts thinking about

Experts suggest that depressed teens get involved in enjoyable activities or hobbies as a means of alleviating the depression.

returning to the track, the thought of putting so much time and effort into the sport may seem too overwhelming, causing him to reject the idea altogether. So, says Mrazek, the boy should not think about anything but "walking one step at a time" and continuing to build from there. He writes: "The idea is to be your own cheerleader, be kind to yourself. You deserve to feel good and to be happy. . . . Set yourself up for success! You can do it!"[67]

Challenging Negativity

Having a positive attitude is valuable for teens with depression —but unfortunately, it is often lacking. Because of the way the illness makes young people feel, they often find themselves mired in negativity, which mental health experts say is one of the most debilitating aspects of depression. In order to overcome it, teens must learn how counterproductive negativity can be and realize that they have to work at changing it. Smith, Segal, and Segal explain: "You can't break out of this pessimistic mind frame by 'just thinking positive.' Happy thoughts or wishful thinking won't cut it. Rather, the trick is to replace negative thoughts with more balanced thoughts."[68]

One of most harmful things depressed teens can do is constantly draw comparisons between themselves and others. Depression erodes their self-image and distorts their perceptions, which can cause them to think everyone they know is happy except for them. Wehrenberg explains: "The negativity of the depressed brain casts a pall over everything, including your self-image. When you're in this negative frame of mind, it can be easy to find examples of people who are doing more or better. But this just reinforces your tendency to see yourself as inadequate or worthless." Wehrenberg adds that depressed teens often engage in such comparisons unconsciously, without even realizing they are doing it. She writes: "You can't stop comparing yourself to others until you notice you are doing it, and once you notice you are doing it, you will probably realize you are doing it a lot."[69] When depressed teens become aware of how destructive such comparisons are, they can learn to focus less on what others are doing and more on their own healing.

Pets Help Teens Cope

It is widely known that pets can help people cope with mental illnesses such as depression. Studies have shown that being around pets helps sufferers feel a sense of emotional connectedness and overall well-being. Although there is no scientific reason for this, psychologist Alan Entin says it can be summed up in two words: "unconditional love." Entin uses the example of dogs always being glad to see their owners even after a short separation. He explains: "When you are feeling down and out, the puppy just starts licking you, being with you, saying with his eyes, 'You are the greatest.' When an animal is giving you that kind of attention, you can't help but respond by improving your mood and playing with it." Along with unconditional love, pets can help keep depression sufferers from feeling alone and isolated. "It relieves their loneliness," Entin says. "People with animals tend to relate to them and they feel better." Another advantage of having pets is that they take the focus off the depression sufferer's problems. Says Entin: "When people have a pet in the house, it forces them to take care of another life." With the focus off themselves, the pet owner may not dwell on his or her depressed mood as much.

Quoted in Kathleen Doheny. "Can Your Depression Problems Improve When You Interact with Your Pet?" WebMD, August 22, 2011. www.webmd.com/depression /recognizing-depression-symptoms/pets-depression.

Studies have shown that pets can help people cope with depression by giving them a sense of being connected to another living thing.

According to the American Academy of Child & Adolescent Psychiatry, the best way for teens to overcome negative thinking is to make a conscious effort to replace it with more realistic, positive thinking. For example, a teen may be so miserable that he or she thinks, "My life is never going to get better." To overcome that self-defeating attitude, teens could train themselves to think, "Okay, I feel like everything is hopeless now, but my life will probably get better if I work at it and get some help." This strategy takes time and effort but can be immensely helpful for those who are mired in what the American Academy of Child & Adolescent Psychiatry calls negative self-talk.

Another strategy for overcoming negativity is to write in a journal. Whenever depressed teens find themselves lapsing into negative thinking, they can jot thoughts down, along with what triggered them, and then put the journal aside. When they are in a better mood, they can review what they wrote. Smith, Segal, and Segal explain: "Consider if the negativity was truly warranted. Ask yourself if there's another way to view the situation. For example, let's say your boyfriend was short with you and you automatically assumed that the relationship was in trouble. But maybe he [was] just having a bad day."[70] Analyzing their journal entries in this way helps teens see how their minds can play tricks on them, causing them to perceive things as worse than they actually are.

Nurturing the Body, Mind, and Spirit

A major factor in coping with depression is for teens to take care of themselves, both physically and emotionally. Unfortunately, however, this is something that those who are depressed often neglect. Research has clearly shown that when young people eat a healthy diet, participate in some kind of regular exercise, and make time to do things that make them happy, depression symptoms are much less severe. Smith, Segal, and Segal explain: "You can make a huge dent in your depression with simple lifestyle changes: exercising every day, . . . eating healthy food instead of the junk you crave, and carving out time for rest and relaxation."[71]

An essential aspect of maintaining a healthy lifestyle is for teens to get enough sleep. The American Academy of Sleep

A Mayo Clinic study found that over 90 percent of teens sleep less than the recommended nine hours per night. Too little sleep can contribute to mood swings and behavioral problems.

Medicine recommends that teens get at least nine hours of sleep per night, but health officials say that is rarely the case. The Mayo Clinic refers to one study that found over 90 percent of teens slept less than the recommended nine hours, and 10 percent slept less than six hours per night. The group explains: "Although this might seem like no big deal, sleep deprivation can have serious consequences. Tired teens can find it difficult to concentrate and learn, or even stay awake

Mental health experts recommend that teens avoid playing video games, listening to loud music, watching television, using computers, or texting before bed because these activities stimulate the mind and can prevent them from falling asleep.

in class. Too little sleep also might contribute to mood swings and behavioral problems."[72]

Columbia University Medical Center researcher James Gangwisch believes that adolescents need more sleep than many people realize. He is studying how sleep deprivation—often the result of late bedtimes and early school start times—can influence teens' moods. In June 2009 Gangwisch announced the findings of a study that focused on the connection between sleep deprivation and depression in teens. He and a team of researchers examined adolescent health surveys completed by over fifteen thousand students in middle school and high school. The team found that the teens whose parents did not require them to be in bed by midnight on school nights were 42 percent more likely to be depressed than teens whose bedtimes were 10 P.M. or earlier. Gangwisch explains: "We feel like we can just eat into our sleep time, but we pay for it in many different ways."[73]

Since depression symptoms are typically more severe when teens do not get enough sleep, they should take steps to develop good nighttime habits. Taking a warm shower before bed is a good winding-down strategy, as is going to bed an hour earlier than usual to read a book. Mental health professionals encourage teens to avoid listening to loud music, playing video games, watching television, or even using computers or text messaging before bed. These are activities that stimulate the mind and can prevent teens from falling asleep. Adolescent psychologist Lisa Boesky explains: "Kids should really be going to bed at the same time every night, getting up at the same time. Pulling all-nighters, staying up all night texting or talking on the phone or on the computer and then catching up on the weekend is not good for the brain."[74]

In the same way that restful sleep can work wonders at helping depressed teens feel better, the same is true of activities that improve fitness. One activity that has proved to help people of all ages with depression is yoga. Although scientists are not certain why yoga is so beneficial, those who practice it often relate to how it improves their concentration, ability to focus, and mood. Because yoga's benefits to the body and mind are so well known, researchers have begun studying it to examine why and how the practice works for people with depression. One theory is that yoga boosts oxygen levels in the brain, which would have the effect of improving mood. Another theory is that yoga boosts levels of the neurotransmitter GABA in the brain. This theory was the subject of a 2010 study by researchers from Boston University.

The Boston University study involved eight people who had been practicing yoga on a regular basis and eleven who were not involved in yoga. At the beginning of the study, the researchers used high-tech MRI imaging to measure GABA levels in the brains of all participants. The yoga group was then

asked to engage in the practice for sixty minutes, while the non-yoga group spent that time reading. A second MRI scan was performed on both groups immediately after the hour was up. The team found a 27 percent increase in GABA levels among those who performed yoga, and no such change in the other group. The findings convinced lead researcher Chris Streeter, who is an assistant professor of psychiatry and neurology at Boston University School of Medicine, that practicing yoga can be of benefit to those who suffer from depression.

A study at Boston University revealed a 27 percent increase in GABA levels among patients who practiced yoga regularly.

She explains: "I am quite sure that this is the first study that's shown that there's a real, measurable change in a major neurotransmitter with a behavioral intervention such as yoga."[75]

Rejecting Unhealthy Ways of Coping

Teens who suffer from depression would benefit immensely by taking up yoga and/or adopting other healthy lifestyle habits, and many do—but others attempt to cope with their illness in unhealthy and even dangerous ways. For instance, an alarming number of depressed teens turn to drugs or alcohol to deal with their emotional pain, which mental health professionals refer to as self-medication. The use of such substances is discouraged because, in addition to being harmful to a teen's health, the effects on his or her mood are temporary and short-lived. Behavioral health researcher and therapist Drew Edwards explains: "People with depression often attempt to lift their mood by taking drugs or drinking. In other words they are 'self-medicating.' This works only for as long as the high lasts. Drugs and alcohol will change your emotions in the short run, but in the long run, they cause additional problems."[76] Even though drugs and alcohol may seem to alleviate depression temporarily, self-medication may actually make the teen's situation worse. Journalist Christine Stapleton, for instance, began drinking to battle her depression as a teenager—an effort to self-medicate that she now describes as futile. Drinking ultimately did not help Stapleton feel better, as she explains: "Alcohol is a depressant; like throwing gasoline on a fire."[77]

The high prevalence of alcohol and drug use among depressed teenagers was revealed in an April 2011 report by the Substance Abuse and Mental Health Services Administration. The researchers who conducted the study found that depressed teens smoked marijuana twice as often as their nondepressed peers, and alcohol use was three times higher among teens with depression. Another study, published in 2008 by the White House Office of National Drug Control Policy, focused specifically on marijuana use among depressed teens. The study found that teens with depression were twice as likely as nondepressed teens to use marijuana and that their

Teens suffering from depression often attempt to lift their mood by self-medicating with alcohol or drugs.

primary reason for using the drug was to alleviate their depressed feelings. The researchers who conducted the study emphasize that teens need to understand how risky that practice can be. As the follow-up report states: "Marijuana and depression are a dangerous combination. In fact, using marijuana can *worsen depression* and lead to more serious mental disorders, such as schizophrenia, anxiety, and even suicide."[78]

"I Have the Willpower"

When teenagers suffer from depression, they may find that life is harder than they ever imagined. Many are plagued by negative thoughts and distorted perceptions about themselves and would rather be alone with their pain and misery than ask for help from others. Depressed teens can learn to cope with their illness, however, and find ways to improve their lives and make themselves feel better. The key is to make healthy lifestyle choices, fight the urge to withdraw from friends and family, and avoid destructive behaviors such as using drugs and alcohol. After suffering from severe depression, Emily Fagan has learned many lessons about how to live a happy, fulfilling life despite her illness. She explains: "My disease will always stick with me. It's not something that will just go away. But I have the tools to control it now, and most of all, I have the willpower."[79]

CHAPTER FIVE

Hope for the Future

Through years of scientific research, public education programs, and screening efforts, the future looks brighter than ever before for teens who suffer from depression or are at risk for developing it. The NIMH and other mental health organizations have devoted tens of millions of dollars to studying depression. In the process, a wealth of information has been gained about risk factors, the role of brain chemistry, and the illness's connection with genetics. At the same time, a growing number of education programs are expanding awareness among teenagers, their parents, health-care providers, and the general public. As these and other efforts continue, scientists hope that fewer teens will have to suffer from depression and its life-altering effects.

Research Revelations

A major priority for scientists studying depression has been searching for ways that teens, especially those with a strong family history of depression, might be prevented from developing it. This was the focus of a study published in 2009 by researchers from Vanderbilt University. Over three hundred adolescents aged thirteen to seventeen were involved in the study and all were considered high risk for developing depression.

The participants had either suffered from the illness in the past or were currently exhibiting symptoms but did not meet the DSM-IV's full criteria for depression. Every teen in the study also had a family history of depression, with one or both parents having suffered from it at some point during their lives.

The participants were assigned to one of two groups. Half were involved in a preventive program that consisted of one ninety-minute cognitive behavioral therapy (CBT) session per week for eight weeks, along with follow-up sessions that continued for six months after the study was complete. The remaining teens formed the control group. Rather than being assigned to any particular type of treatment, they were free to seek help from community resources of their choosing.

Teens undergoing cognitive behavioral therapy are taught to think more realistically about their problems and experiences and to recognize and avoid negative thinking patterns.

The teens involved in the CBT sessions were taught to think more realistically about their problems and experiences and to recognize and avoid negative thinking. This approach is known as the ABCD model, which stands for *A*ctivating event, *B*eliefs and thoughts about the event, perceived *C*onsequences of the event, and *D*isputing negative thoughts and assumptions. Guided by a social worker or other professional trained in CBT, study participants talked about an activating event such as a breakup with a boyfriend or girlfriend. Next they explored their typical beliefs about the occurrence, such as thinking, "It's all my fault." When considering perceived consequences, the teens were likely to have a negative thought such as, "I'll never find another boyfriend or girlfriend." The D phase was the most critical because after the teens had exhibited negative thinking, they learned to challenge and replace it. For example, rather than focusing on negativity, they might train themselves to think, "Am I being realistic? Would other people see this the same way I do?"

The researchers followed the teens' progress for nine months. At the conclusion of the study, it was clear that those in the CBT group had made significant strides in overcoming negative thinking, which meant they had reduced their risk for depression. This appeared to be true when only 21 percent of those teens went on to develop the illness, compared with 33 percent of teens in the control group. For the CBT group participants whose parents were not currently suffering from depression, the results were even more dramatic—only 11.7 percent had a depressive episode during the nine-month follow-up period. Anne Marie Albano, a psychologist who directs Columbia University Medical Center's Clinic for Anxiety and Related Disorders, says the Vanderbilt study "really moves the field forward." According to Albano, additional studies confirm that rates of mental illness have increased among young people, which has sounded the alarm for the need to intervene at an early stage to prevent teen depression. She explains: "This study is telling us that if you get kids early in the cycle of depression when they have symptoms and are on the path, you can give them skills that manage those symptoms."[80]

Along with research devoted to preventing depression among teens, another focus has been on developing better treatments for those who suffer from it. Multiple studies have revealed the tremendous potential of a drug known as ketamine, which is currently used as an anesthetic in human and veterinary medicine. The reason scientists are so enthusiastic about ketamine is that it has been effective in 70 percent of treatment-resistant patients, meaning those who do not respond to conventional depression treatment. Also, ketamine has proved to relieve depression symptoms within a day, and sometimes after only a few hours, which is a much shorter period of time than with antidepressants that are currently available. Speaking of one of the ketamine studies, psychiatrist David Feifel explains: "What is really exciting is that the response [to the drug] was very rapid. . . . This is not something we are used to seeing in this difficult-to-treat population." As promising as ketamine is, however, there are challenges associated with its use. At this point the drug can only be given intravenously, or injected directly into a patient's vein, which means it is not a practical treatment for most depression sufferers. Also, according to the NIMH, ketamine carries the risk of side effects such as nausea, vomiting, dizziness, and loss of appetite.

Because of the challenges, ketamine is not officially sanctioned as a depression treatment. It is, however, used under controlled circumstances at some medical facilities with treatment-resistant patients who believe that the benefits outweigh the risks. Feifel explains: "We have a population of patients who have no other option; they are extremely ill, their lives are miserable; they have tried everything."[81] These depression sufferers are given ketamine injections on a regular basis. Although the drug has been extremely effective for them, the effects are not long lasting, which is another problem that is yet to be solved. But because of the potential benefits of ketamine, scientists are committed to further research on the drug's effects, in the hope of eventually ironing out the difficulties and making the drug more suitable for larger numbers of depression sufferers. Feifel is convinced that this is a distinct possibility in the not-too-distant future.

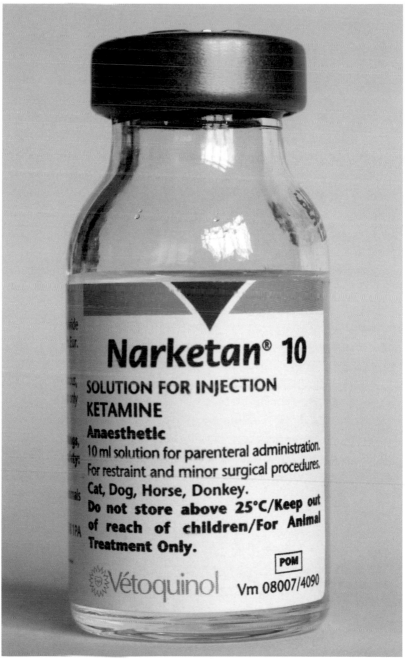

An anesthetic used in veterinary and human medicine, the drug ketamine has been found to be effective in treating 70 percent of depression patients previously resistant to treatment.

Turning Grief into Action

In 2009 Victoria Bennis was trying to pick up the pieces of her life in the wake of the tragic suicide of her sixteen-year-old brother, John. When another teenage boy from the same town committed suicide the following May, Bennis knew that she had to do something. So she and a friend founded Save A Life, an organization whose mission is to raise awareness about the problem of teen suicide, educate communities, and let troubled teenagers know that they should reach out for help if they feel depressed and/or suicidal. Says Bennis: "I couldn't change the past for my brother. But I want to be there for other kids. These kids are obviously so tormented inside, and they think they can't ask for help. But they can."

Save A Life raises money to further its cause through community events such as 5K walks. All proceeds raised from such events go toward sponsoring training programs for parents and teachers, who learn how to spot depression warning signs, educate teens about the importance of asking for support, and get young people the help they need. During a Save A Life walkathon held in September 2011, three hundred people participated, and over five thousand dollars was raised. Bennis is confident that as awareness of her program continues to grow, more people will become involved, more money will be raised, and in the process, young lives will be saved.

Quoted in Sadia Latifi. "Preventing Suicides Is Fundraiser's Aim." *Cary (NC) News*, September 7, 2010. www.carynews.com/2010 /09/07 /20285/preventing-suicides-is-fundraisers.html.

Save A Life raises money to further its cause through hosting community events such as walkathons.

"One Classroom at a Time"

As research continues to yield promising new findings about depression, a growing number of education programs are expanding public awareness about the illness and its associated risks. One program that is nationally recognized for its success rate is known as the Adolescent Depression Awareness Program (ADAP), whose mission is to raise awareness of teen depression "one classroom at a time." Created by Johns Hopkins Hospital in 1999 in the wake of several teen suicides, ADAP is a three-hour curriculum-based program for high school students, teachers, and parents nationwide. It includes interactive lectures and discussions, videos of teens describing their experiences with depression, group activities, and homework assignments. Some of the key messages include how to identify symptoms of depression, how to recognize parallels between depression and other medical illnesses, and that suicide is a needless consequence of the illness that can be avoided if teens are evaluated and treated. The authors of the program brochure write: "ADAP's message is hopeful, emphasizing the importance of treatment and seeking help. The curriculum stresses the need to share concerns with a parent, teacher or counselor so that appropriate action can be taken."[82]

Since ADAP was launched, it has grown from 530 participants in 1999 to over 22,500 today. Wherever the program has been implemented, it has proved to make a significant difference in depression awareness among students. Its success has been measured with ongoing analyses by ADAP team leaders, who test participating students' knowledge before they start the program and again six weeks later. In one analysis of a large public school district in Maryland, only one-fifth of students scored 80 percent or higher at the beginning of the program—and by the time it was completed, that number had more than tripled. Says Johns Hopkins psychiatrist Karen L. Swartz, who is the director of ADAP:

> Based on recent feedback from participating teachers, parents, and students, the ADAP program has been very well received by school communities. Educators at schools have

noted that the information contained within the curriculum is valuable and essential. The program not only offers a better medical understanding and awareness of adolescent depression and mood disorders, it also offers hope and reassurance that treatment options are available.[83]

TeenScreen Primary Care provides health-care professionals with free screening tools to assist them in evaluating whether their adolescent patients are suffering from depression, anxiety, or other conditions and to assess their risk of suicide.

Going forward, the ADAP team will continue reaching out to classrooms to let depressed kids know that they do not have to suffer in silence.

Crucial Depression Screening

An important component of ADAP and other education programs is screening teens for depression at an early stage, before symptoms develop. These screenings are the recommendation of a national panel of experts known as the U.S. Preventive Services Task Force. In March 2009 the group issued a statement that all adolescents aged twelve to eighteen should be screened for depression when systems are in place to ensure accurate diagnosis, psychotherapy, and follow-up. In addition to being endorsed by a government health organization, medical research has shown that the use of screening to detect early symptoms and warning signs for depression is an important tool in the fight against teen depression.

One screening program, which was developed by Columbia University's Division of Child and Adolescent Psychiatry, is known as TeenScreen. It is a privately funded public health initiative whose aim is to increase youth access to regular mental health checkups and improve the early identification of depression and other mental illnesses. The program has two components: TeenScreen Primary Care, which is designed to assist health-care professionals with integrating mental health screening into routine medical checkups for adolescents, and TeenScreen Schools and Communities, a community-based effort in which mental health screening is available to young people through more than seventeen hundred sites located in forty-six U.S. states.

TeenScreen Primary Care provides physicians and other health-care professionals with free screening tools to assist them in evaluating whether their adolescent patients are suffering from depression, anxiety, or other conditions and to assess whether they are at risk for suicide. The mental health checkup component is designed for adolescents aged eleven to eighteen and involves a simple screening procedure completed through a brief questionnaire. The evaluation is intended to be incorporated into routine well-child examinations, diagnostic and treatment exams, sports physicals, or other types of office visits.

The priority of TeenScreen Schools and Communities is to make adolescent mental health and well-being a national priority, while ensuring that all parents are given the opportunity to have their teens receive mental health checkups. The program requires parental consent and uses a questionnaire and interview process to determine whether a teenager may be at risk for depression, other mental illnesses, and/or suicide. If a teen is determined to be at risk, parents are notified and helped to identify and connect with local services where they can obtain a complete evaluation by a mental health professional.

Focus on Suicide Prevention

One of the primary reasons that TeenScreen and other screening programs were developed is to reduce the risk of teen suicide, as research has shown a close connection between suicide and depression. In the United States suicide is the third leading cause of death for adolescents, after homicides and accidental injuries. Health officials stress that the majority of teens who take their own lives suffered from depression, and this risk could be markedly reduced if young people take any mention of suicide by their peers seriously. According to Mental Health America, four out of five teens who attempt suicide have given clear warnings ahead of time—but too often these warnings are brushed off and not taken seriously. Adolescent psychologist Lisa Boesky explains: "When a youth makes a suicide attempt almost always they have told a friend. Very rarely have they told a parent or an adult in their life." Boesky emphasizes that it is essential for teens to recognize warning signs and to realize that they must not hesitate to speak up if someone even hints about suicide. She explains: "It's no different than if you see someone with a gun at school or you hear someone talking about blowing up the school, schools are very good at having kids report that. We need to do the same thing with suicide, and we haven't yet. There is a lot of resistance and a lot of misunderstanding but it would make a world of difference."[84]

A Promising Discovery

It can be extremely challenging for physicians to diagnose depression in teenagers. There are no diagnostic tests for the disorder, so doctors must make determinations based on a teen's description of symptoms. That may change, though, because of the findings of a study published in April 2012. A team of researchers from Northwestern University's Feinberg School of Medicine concluded that a simple blood test can distinguish between young people who suffer from depression and those who do not.

The goal of the study was to identify distinct molecules (known as biomarkers) in the bloodstream that could indicate the presence of depression. The research team first performed an experiment with laboratory rats, half of which were bred to have depression and half of which were healthy. The team identified eleven biomarkers in blood samples from the depressed rats but did not find these biomarkers in the blood of the healthy rats. In a second experiment the team took blood samples from twenty-eight teenagers, half of whom had been diagnosed with depression. An analysis showed the same eleven biomarkers in the blood of the depressed teens but not the healthy teens, which confirmed the researchers' theory that signs of depression are evident in the blood. According to lead researcher Eva Redei, this study proves that blood tests will eventually be able to diagnose depression, which could lead to earlier treatment and better outcomes for patients.

Researchers from Northwestern University's Feinberg School of Medicine have discovered that a simple blood test may eventually determine whether a teen suffers from depression.

Taking a suicide threat seriously saved the life of a sixteen-year-old boy from Britain. He had developed an online friendship with an American girl his own age, and one night during the spring of 2009 they were chatting on Facebook via instant messaging. The boy wrote: "I'm going away to do something I've been thinking about for a while then everyone will find out."[85] Fearing that he intended to kill himself, the girl told her mother, who then called the state police. This sparked an international string of emergency messages that traveled from the United States to Britain's Scotland Yard and finally to local police in the boy's hometown. It took a great deal of effort to pinpoint his exact location, but investigators were able to track down his address. Police and emergency responders raced to his home, where he was discovered barely conscious after taking an overdose of drugs. They rushed the boy to the hospital, where doctors were able to save his life, and his Facebook friend was hailed for her efforts to save him.

The growing publicity of teen suicide has sparked numerous awareness and prevention programs. One that has proved to be immensely successful is called Surviving the Teens, which was developed by Cincinnati Children's Hospital and Medical Center. The program's focus is on educating students about the warning signs of suicide, either in themselves or their friends, and letting them know where they can get access to help. Surviving the Teens consists of three components: student training, a program designed for parents, and "gatekeeper training" for school staff and community members.

As part of an effort to assess the program's effectiveness, suicide prevention expert Cathy Strunk taught Surviving the Teens to over six thousand high school students during the 2008–2009 school year. Prior to the study, Strunk and her colleagues surveyed over nine hundred of the teens to gauge their knowledge of depression and suicide risk. Three months later, when the program was complete, the teaching team surveyed four hundred of those participants to compare the knowledge they had gained with their responses on the previous test—and the results were impressive. The number of students who had reported considering suicide dropped 65 percent, those who actually planned to commit suicide dropped 48 percent, and those who attempted suicide dropped 67 percent. Another finding was that the number of students who had reported feeling sad and hopeless prior to the study decreased from 22.6 percent to 16.8 percent. Strunk shares her thoughts about what the teen participants gained from the program: "The overwhelming majority of students felt Surviving the Teens helped them to learn suicide warning signs, suicide and depression risk factors, how to effectively cope with stress, steps to take if they or a friend felt suicidal, and how to talk to their parents and friends about their problems."[86]

Teens Helping Teens

Research has shown that one of the most effective methods of spreading information about teen depression and the associated risk of suicide is for young people to personally share their own experiences. One example is Kirk Zajac, who volunteers with the Suicide Prevention Education Alliance and visits high schools throughout northeastern Ohio. When he is in front of audiences, Zajac talks candidly about his own difficult struggle with depression and encourages others who are suffering to reach out for help. Olivia Thompson also uses her experience to benefit other teens. She talks about her battle with depression, how she was misdiagnosed when she first sought help from a psychologist, and how hard she fought to recover. She also shares the desperate point she reached before being treated, as she explains: "I realized I didn't really care if I died. I wouldn't try to kill myself, but if I died, I wouldn't care." Olivia makes it clear to teens that there is help available for them, and they should not—under any circumstances—remain silent if they are suffering. She explains: "I know there are other teens like me, going through the same thing. I just want there to be more awareness."[87]

Jordan Burnham is another teen with a depression-related experience to share with teens—and he is very fortunate to be alive and able to talk about it. When Burnham was fifteen years old, he was diagnosed with depression. Even though he was a star athlete, very popular with his classmates, and an excellent

Pennsylvania judge John B. Leete was a leader in bringing the Yellow Ribbon Suicide Prevention program to his county. In the program, teens reach out to peers who show the warning signs of suicidal thinking.

student, he still felt like he was a disappointment to himself and his parents. By the time he was a senior, his emotional pain was so overwhelming that Burnham felt he had no reason to live, and he attempted suicide by leaping from his bedroom window. After falling over 100 feet (30.48m) to the ground, his body was broken—but he survived, and today he believes that his life was spared for a reason. Burnham has made it his mission to use his experience to help other teens who might also be suffering from depression. He volunteers for an organization known as Active Minds and travels to high schools and colleges throughout the United States, where he shares tales of his personal struggle with depression and offers hope to others. After one of his presentations at a high school in Pennsylvania, a school official stated: "Jordan comes in and you can hear a pin drop. He's 19 years old. Kids listen to kids."[88]

There Is Always Hope

Awareness of teen depression has grown immensely since the 1970s, when it was widely believed that the illness did not affect young people. Scientists have devoted many years to studying depression, and mental health professionals have made a concerted effort to educate teens about it, help them understand that it is a highly treatable illness, and let them know that there is help available if they need it. Research has yielded promising findings about improved drugs to treat depression, as well as how teens who are screened early could potentially avoid developing the illness. With all this progress, and more that is surely to come, there is every reason to hope that teen depression will be far less prevalent in the future than it is today.

Notes

Introduction: Trapped in Darkness

1. Dore Frances. "Teen Depression Increases as the New School Year Starts." *Dr. Dore Frances PhD* (blog), WordPress .com, August 28, 2011. http://drdorefrancesphd.wordpress .com/2011/08/28/teen-depression-increases-as-the-new-school-year-starts.
2. Quoted in Terri Finch Hamilton. "Teen Who Suffered Depression Wants Peers to Know: This Can Happen to Anybody." *Grand Rapids (MI) Press*, September 25, 2011. www.mlive.com/health/index.ssf/2011/09/teen_who_suffered _depression _w.html.
3. Quoted in Hamilton. "Teen Who Suffered Depression Wants Peers to Know."
4. Quoted in Hamilton. "Teen Who Suffered Depression Wants Peers to Know."
5. Quoted in Hamilton. "Teen Who Suffered Depression Wants Peers to Know."
6. Quoted in Hamilton. "Teen Who Suffered Depression Wants Peers to Know."

Chapter One: What Is Depression?

7. Wes Burgess. *The Depression Answer Book*. Naperville, IL: Sourcebooks, 2009, p. 4.
8. Burgess. *The Depression Answer Book*, p. 2.
9. Burgess. *The Depression Answer Book*, p. 2.
10. Burgess. *The Depression Answer Book*, p. 3.
11. National Institute of Mental Health. *Depression in Children and Adolescents Fact Sheet*. April 25, 2011. www .nimh.nih.gov/health/publications/depression-in-children-and -adolescents/depression-in-children-and-adolescents.pdf.
12. National Alliance on Mental Illness. *Understanding Bipolar Disorder and Recovery*, August 2008. www.nami.org

/Template.cfm?Section=By_Illness&template=/ContentManage
ment/ContentDisplay.cfm&ContentID=67728.

13. Quoted in Elena Ferrarin. "Aurora Teen Overcomes Severe
Depression." *Arlington Heights (IL) Daily Herald,* May 16,
2011.www.dailyherald.com/article/20110516/news/705169977.

14. American Academy of Child & Adolescent Psychiatry. "Your
Adolescent—Depressive Disorders," 2010. www.aacap
.org/cs/root/publication_store/your_adolescent_depressive
_disorders.

15. National Institutes of Health. "Postpartum Depression."
MedlinePlus, April 28, 2011. www.nlm.nih.gov/medline
plus/postpartumdepression.html.

16. Amal Chakraburtty, reviewer. "Seasonal Affective Disorder
(SAD)." WebMD, January 26, 2009. http://teens.webmd.com
/seasonal-affective-disorder?page=2.

17. John M. Grohol. "What's the Difference Between Depression and Manic Depression?" Psych Central, September 22,
2010. http://psychcentral.com/lib/2009/whats-the-difference
-between-depression-and-manic-depression.

18. National Institute of Mental Health. *Bipolar Disorder in
Children and Teens,* October 12, 2011. www.nimh.nih.gov
/health/publications/bipolar-disorder-in-children-and-teens-
easy-to-read/complete-index.shtml.

19. National Alliance on Mental Illness. *Understanding Bipolar Disorder and Recovery.*

20. Mayo Clinic. "Cyclothymia (Cyclothymic Disorder)," April
16, 2010. www.mayoclinic.com/health/cyclothymia/DS00
729/DSECTION=symptoms.

21. Quoted in Maureen Cavanaugh. "Teens and Depression."
KBPS, June 3, 2010. www.kpbs.org/news/2010/jun/03/teens-
and-depression.

22. Harvard Medical School. "Depression in Children and
Teenagers," 2011. www.health.harvard.edu/newsweek/
Depression_in_Children_and_Teenagers.htm.

23. National Institute of Mental Health. "How Does Depression
Affect Adolescent Girls?" January 21, 2009. www.nimh.nih
.gov/health/publications/women-and-depression-discovering
-hope/how-does-depression-affect-adolescent-girls.shtml.

24. Cecilia A. Essau and Weining C. Chang. Epidemiology, Co-morbidity, and Course of Adolescent Depression. In *Treatments for Adolescent Depression: Theory and Practice*, edited by Cecilia A. Essau. Oxford: Oxford University Press. March 16, 2009. http://fds.oup.com/www.oup.com /pdf/13 /97801 99226504_chapter1.pdf.

25. Roy H. Lubit. "Posttraumatic Stress Disorder in Children." Medscape, April 20, 2011. http://emedicine.medscape.com/ article/918844-overview.

Chapter Two: Causes of Depression in Teens

26. Kenneth Duckworth, Darcy Gruttadaro, and Dana Markley. *What Families Need to Know About Adolescent Depression.* National Alliance on Mental Illness, December 2010. www.nami .org/Content/ContentGroups/CAAC/FamilyGuidePRINT.pdf.

27. Michael Waldholz. "Depression May Originate in Our Genes." HealthyPlace, July 31, 2003. www.healthyplace .com/depression/main/depression-may-originate-in-our-genes /menu-id-68.

28. Scicurious. "SfN Neuroblogging: SERT-anly Slower, the Flinders Sensitive Line Model of Depression." *The Scicurious Brain* (blog), *Scientific American*, November 15, 2011. http://blogs.scientificamerican.com/scicurious-brain /2011/11/15/sfn-neuroblogging-sert-anly-slower-the-flinders -sensitive-line-model-of-depression.

29. Quoted in ScienceDaily. "Critical Brain Chemical Shown to Play Role in Severe Depression," March 1, 2010. www.science daily.com/releases/2010/03/100301102803.htm.

30. National Institute of Mental Health. "Brain Chemical Linked to Joylessness Provides Insight into Teen Depression," October 6, 2011. www.nimh.nih.gov/science-news /2011/brain-chemical-linked-to-joylessness-provides-insight -into-teen-depression.shtml.

31. Quoted in ScienceDaily. "Biological Links Found Between Childhood Abuse and Adolescent Depression," April 20, 2011. www.sciencedaily.com/releases/2011/04/110420125506.htm.

32. American Academy of Child & Adolescent Psychiatry. "Your Adolescent—Depressive Disorders."

33. Quoted in Lisa Belkin. "Depression in Teenagers." *Motherlode* (blog), *New York Times*, March 18, 2010. http://parenting.blogs.nytimes.com/2010/03/18/depression-in-teens.
34. Quoted in Cathy Cassinos-Carr. "Health: Teen Depression." *Sacramento*, May 2011. www.sacmag.com/Sacramento-Magazine/May-2011/Teen-Depression.
35. Quoted in Cassinos-Carr. "Health."
36. Quoted in *USA Today*. "Study: Students More Stressed Now than During Depression?" January 12, 2010. www.usatoday.com/news/education/2010-01-12-students-depression-anxiety_N.htm.
37. Mental Health America. "Depression in Teens," 2011. http://nmha.org/index.cfm?objectid=C7DF950F-1372-4D20-C8B5BD8DFDD94CF1.
38. Quoted in Ferrarin. "Aurora Teen Overcomes Severe Depression."
39. Jean-Marie Bruzzese. "Depression in Children and Adolescents with a Chronic Disease." NYU Child Study Center. www.aboutourkids.org/articles/depression_in_children_adolescents_chronic_disease.
40. Amal Chakraburtty, reviewer. "Coping with Chronic Illnesses and Depression." WebMD, September 12, 2009. www.webmd.com/depression/guide/chronic-illnesses-depression.
41. Quoted in Serena Gordon. "Teens with Epilepsy Prone to Depression." HealingWell.com, March 30, 2006. http://news.healingwell.com/index.php?p=news1&id=531881.

Chapter Three: Diagnosis and Treatment

42. Quoted in Teri Robert. "Teen Depression—an Interview." My Depression Connection. HealthCentral, August 31, 2009. www.healthcentral.com/depression/teens-304402-5_pf.html.
43. Substance Abuse and Mental Health Services Administration. "Major Depressive Episode and Treatment Among Adolescents: 2009." *The NSDUH Report*, April 28, 2011. http://oas.samhsa.gov/2k11/009/AdolescentDepressionHTML.pdf.
44. Therese J. Borchard. "8 Tips for Teenage Depression." Psych Central, May 27, 2011. http://psychcentral.com/blog/archives/2011/05/27/8-tips-for-teenage-depression.

45. National Alliance on Mental Illness. *Depression in Children and Adolescents Fact Sheet,* October 2009. www.nami .org/Template.cfm?Section=Depression&Template=/Content Management/ContentDisplay.cfm&ContentID=89198.
46. American Academy of Child & Adolescent Psychiatry. "Your Adolescent—Depressive Disorders."
47. Dartmouth Medical School. *Teen Depression: Cognitive Behavioral Therapy,* 2011. www.dartmouthcoopproject.org /TeenMental/Flyers/Parents/CognitiveBehavioral_PT.pdf.
48. Dartmouth Medical School. *Teen Depression.*
49. Quoted in Beth W. Orenstein. "Depression Treatment: Talking It Out." EverydayHealth.com, May 21, 2010. www.every dayhealth.com/health-report/living-well-with-depression/talking -it-out.aspx.
50. Quoted in Hamilton. "Teen Who Suffered Depression Wants Peers to Know."
51. Pamela Broderick and Christina Weston. "Family Therapy with a Depressed Adolescent." *Innovations in Clinical Neuroscience,* January 2009. www.innovationscns.com /family-therapy-with-a-depressed-adolescent.
52. Quoted in Broderick and Weston. "Family Therapy with a Depressed Adolescent."
53. American Academy of Child & Adolescent Psychiatry. "FAQs on Child and Adolescent Depression." www.aacap .org/cs/child_and_adolescent_depression_resource_center /faqs_on_child_and_adolescent_depression.
54. National Institute of Mental Health. "Questions and Answers About the NIMH Treatment for Adolescents with Depression Study (TADS)," March 18, 2010. www.nimh.nih .gov/trials/practical/tads/questions-and-answers-about-the- nimh-treatment-for-adolescents-with-depression-study-tads .shtml.
55. American Academy of Child & Adolescent Psychiatry. "FAQs on Child and Adolescent Depression."
56. Borchard. "8 Tips for Teenage Depression."
57. Quoted in Caroline Cassels. "More Evidence Confirms Diet's Link to Mental Health." Medscape, October 14, 2011. www.medscape.com/viewarticle/751533.

58. American Psychological Association. "Exercise Helps Keep Your Psyche Fit," May 28, 2004. www.apa.org/research /action/fit.aspx.
59. Quoted in Laura Blue. "Is Exercise the Best Drug for Depression?" *Time*, June 19, 2010. www.time.com/time /health/article/0,8599,1998021,00.html.
60. Mental Health America. "Depression in Teens."

Chapter Four: Living with Depression
61. Melinda Smith, Robert Segal, and Jeanne Segal. "Dealing with Depression." Helpguide.org, October 2011. http://help guide.org/mental/depression_tips.htm.
62. Quoted in Kathryn Baker. "What to Look for in Teen Depression." Ideastream, June 14, 2010. www.ideastream .org/news/feature/29257.
63. Margaret Wehrenberg. *The 10 Best-Ever Depression Management Techniques*. New York: Norton, 2010, p. 139.
64. Carol Glod. "Teen Depression." Families for Depression Awareness. www.familyaware.org/expertprofiles/194-dr-carol -glod-teen-depression.html.
65. Quoted in Seo Hee Koh. "Teenagers Dealing with Depression." HealthyPlace, January 4, 2009. www.healthyplace .com/depression/children/teenagers-dealing-with-depression /menu-id-68.
66. Suzanne Barston, Melinda Smith, and Jeanne Segal. "Dealing with Teen Depression." Helpguide.org, October 2011. http://helpguide.org/mental/depression_teen_teenagers.htm.
67. David Mrazek. "Recover from Depression One Step at a Time." *Depression* (blog), Mayo Clinic, June 25, 2008. www .mayoclinic.com/health/depression-blog/MY00092.
68. Smith, Segal, and Segal. "Dealing with Depression."
69. Wehrenberg. *The 10 Best-Ever Depression Management Techniques*, p. 77.
70. Smith, Segal, and Segal. "Dealing with Depression."
71. Smith, Segal, and Segal. "Dealing with Depression."
72. Mayo Clinic. "Teen Sleep: Why Is Your Teen So Tired?" August 4, 2011. www.mayoclinic.com/health/teens-health/CC 00019.

73. Quoted in Greg Toppo. "Study Links Teen Depression to Bedtimes." *USA Today*, October 2, 2009. www.usatoday .com/news/health/2009-06-09-bedtime-teen-depression_N.htm.

74. Quoted in Cavanaugh. "Teens and Depression."

75. Quoted in E.J. Mundell. "Yoga May Help Treat Depression, Anxiety Disorders." ABC News, June 7, 2010. http://abc news.go.com/Health/Healthday/story?id=4507486&page=1 #.Tt-VfFawWRE.

76. Drew Edwards. "Alarming Trends in Teen Substance Abuse and Depression." Achieve Solutions, March 25, 2011. www .achievesolutions.net/achievesolutions/en/Content.do?content Id=22386.

77. Christine Stapleton. "Depression, Alcohol and My Poor Little Teenage Brain." *Depression on My Mind* (blog), Psych Central, May 2010. http://blogs.psychcentral.com/depression /2010/05/depression-alcohol-and-my-poor-little-teenag -brain.

78. Office of National Drug Control Policy. *Teen Marijuana Use Worsens Depression*, May 2008. www.theantidrug.com /pdfs/teen-marijuana-depression-report.pdf.

79. Quoted in Ferrarin. "Aurora Teen Overcomes Severe Depression."

Chapter Five: Hope for the Future

80. Quoted in Claudia Wallis. "Study: Early Therapy Can Save Teens from Depression." *Time*, June 4, 2009. www.time .com/time/health/article/0,8599,1902500,00.html.

81. David Feifel. "Is Ketamine a Game Changer?" Medscape, January 26, 2011. www.medscape.com/viewarticle/736133.

82. Johns Hopkins Medicine. *A Decade of Raising Awareness One Classroom at a Time*. www.hopkinsmedicine.org/ psychiatry/specialty_areas/moods/ADAP/images/ADAP_ Program _Summary.pdf.

83. Karen L. Swartz. "Adolescent Depression Awareness Program (ADAP)." Mental Health Association in Delaware, 2009. www.mhainde.org/edADAP.asp.

84. Quoted in Cavanaugh. "Teens and Depression."

85. Quoted in Patrick Sawer. "Suicidal Teenager Saved by Facebook Friend." *Telegraph* (London), April 4, 2009. www

.telegraph.co.uk/technology/facebook/5104882/Suicidal-teen
ager-saved-by-Facebook-friend.html.
86. Quoted in ScienceDaily. "Program Helps High School Students Overcome Depression and Thoughts of Suicide," August 12, 2011. www.sciencedaily.com/releases/2011/08/1108
12102742.htm.
87. Quoted in Hamilton. "Teen Who Suffered Depression Wants
Peers to Know."
88. Quoted in Brandie Kessler. "Bringing a Dark Subject to
Light." *Pottstown (PA) Mercury*, March 22, 2009. www
.pottsmerc.com/articles/2009/03/22/news/srv0000004941300
.txt?viewmode=2.

Glossary

anhedonia: A condition that involves the inability to experience pleasure.

cognitive behavioral therapy (CBT): A type of psychotherapy that is focused on modifying behavior; specifically, changing unhealthy patterns of thinking.

comorbidity: The coexistence of two or more illnesses.

cortisol: A hormone produced by the body in response to stress, anger, or fear.

delusions: Strange, irrational beliefs that have no basis in reality.

dysthymia: A form of depression that is milder than major depression, but whose symptoms last for longer than a year.

gamma-aminobutyric acid (GABA): A neurotransmitter that plays an essential role in brain functions such as moods, thoughts, and actions.

hallucinations: The state of hearing and/or seeing things that do not actually exist.

hypomania: A milder form of mania.

magnetic resonance imaging (MRI): A diagnostic technique that uses a magnetic field and pulses of radio wave energy to form pictures of organs and structures inside the body.

mania: Bouts of exaggerated euphoria and excitability that are also called manic episodes.

mood disorders: A group of mental illnesses that involve severe disturbances in a person's emotional state, or mood.

neuron: A nerve cell.

neurotransmitters: Chemicals in the brain that help neurons communicate with each other.

serotonin: A neurotransmitter that is critical for functions such as sleep, pain, memory, and mood.

Organizations to Contact

Centre for Clinical Interventions
223 James St.
Northbridge, Western Australia 6003
Phone: (08) 9227 4399; Fax: (08) 9328 5911
Website: www.cci.health.wa.gov.au

The Centre for Clinical Interventions is an educational, research, and treatment organization that helps people with depression and other mood disorders. Its website offers a wealth of information about depression, including a collection of downloadable workbooks.

Depression and Bipolar Support Alliance
730 N. Franklin St., Suite 501
Chicago, IL 60654-7225
Phone: (800) 826-3632; Fax: (312) 642-7243
Website: www.dbsalliance.org

The Depression and Bipolar Support Alliance seeks to improve the lives of people living with depression and bipolar disorder through research, education, and support. Its website offers a comprehensive "Learn About Mood Disorders" section, as well as frequently asked questions, statistics, and information about recovery.

Families for Depression Awareness
395 Totten Pond Rd., Suite 404
Waltham, MA 02451
Phone: (781) 890-0220; Fax: (781) 890-2411
Website: www.familyaware.org

Families for Depression Awareness supports families by helping them recognize and manage the various forms of depression and other mood disorders. Its website offers depression statistics, personal stories and interviews, and a special "Teens/Kids" section.

Mental Health America
2000 N. Beauregard St., 6th Floor
Alexandria, VA 22311
Phone: (703) 684-7722; toll-free: (800) 969-6642
Fax: (703) 684-5968
Website: www.nmha.org

Mental Health America is dedicated to helping people live mentally healthier lives and educating the public about mental health and mental illness. Its website search engine produces numerous articles about teen depression that address warning signs, causes, risks, and treatment options.

Minding Your Mind Foundation
42 W. Lancaster Ave., 2nd Floor
Ardmore, PA 19003
Phone: (610) 642-3879; Fax: (610) 896-5704
Website: www.mindingyourmind.org

The Minding Your Mind Foundation provides mental health education to teenagers and seeks to decrease the stigma attached to mental illness. Its website offers a number of articles about depression and other mental health–related issues, as well as personal stories of teens who understand the turmoil of depression after living through it and recovering.

National Alliance on Mental Illness (NAMI)
3803 N. Fairfax Dr., Suite 100
Arlington, VA 22203
Phone: (703) 524-7600; toll-free (800) 950-6264
Fax: (703) 524-9094
Website: www.nami.org

The NAMI is dedicated to improving the lives of people who suffer from mental illness, as well as the lives of their families. Numerous articles about teen depression can be obtained through the website's search engine.

National Institute of Mental Health (NIMH)
Science Writing, Press, and Dissemination Branch
6001 Executive Blvd., Room 8184, MSC 9663
Bethesda, MD 20892-9663
Phone: (301) 443-4513; toll-free: (866) 615-6464;
Fax: (301) 443-4279
Website: www.nimh.nih.gov

The NIMH is the largest scientific organization in the world specializing in mental illness research and the promotion of health. Teens can find much information on its website, including numerous articles about depression, statistics, and research findings.

notMYkid
5230 E. Shea Blvd., Suite 100
Scottsdale, AZ 85254
Phone: (602) 652-0163
Website: www.notmykid.org

notMYkid is a nonprofit organization that is devoted to helping teens and parents cope with depression and other mental health conditions. The website's "Hot Topics" section on depression offers facts, warning signs and symptoms, and links to current and archived articles.

Suicide Prevention Education Alliance
29425 Chagrin Blvd., Suite 306
Cleveland, OH 44122-4637
Phone: (216) 464-3471; Fax: (216) 464-3108
Website: www.speaneohio.org

The Suicide Prevention Education Alliance seeks to educate young people about depression and the warning signs of suicide and encourages them to seek professional help for themselves or others. Its website offers information about depression, how it is linked to substance abuse and suicide, and survivor stories.

For More Information

Books

Bev Cobain. *When Nothing Matters Anymore*. Minneapolis, MN: Free Spirit, 2007. This book was written especially for depressed teens by the cousin of Nirvana lead singer Kurt Cobain, who suffered from severe depression and took his own life in 1994.

Cait Irwin, Dwight L. Evans, and Linda Wasmer Andrews. *Monochrome Days: A First-Hand Account of One Teenager's Experience with Depression*. New York: Oxford University Press, 2007. Written by a young woman who was stricken with depression when she was fourteen years old, this book is the story of pain, suffering, family support, hope, and recovery.

Allen R. Miller. *Living with Depression*. New York: Facts On File, 2008. This book helps teens understand depression by discussing warning signs, diagnosis and treatment, and ways to help themselves, friends, or family members who are depressed.

Lisa Schab. *Beyond the Blues: A Workbook to Help Teens Overcome Depression*. Oakland, CA: Instant Help, 2008. This book is designed to help depressed teens learn how to cope with sad and difficult feelings, find new ways to make friends, and deal with conflicts.

Faye Zucker and Joan E. Huebl. *Beating Depression: Teens Find Light at the End of the Tunnel*. New York: Franklin Watts, 2007. This book offers real-life stories of how teens struggled with and recovered from depression.

Periodicals

Sarah Wassner Flynn. "Coming Out of the Darkness." *Girls' Life*, December 2008/January 2009.

John Keilman. "Fragile Teen Is Saved by Caring and Luck."
Seattle Times, September 20, 2010.
Claudia Wallis. "Early Therapy Can Save Teens from Depression." *Time*, June 4, 2009.

Internet Sources

Karen A. "Held Down by Depression." *L.A. Youth,* September 2011.
www.layouth.com/held-down-by-depression/#storybreak.
Suzanne Barston, Melinda Smith, and Jeanne Segal. "Dealing
with Teen Depression: Tips and Tools for Helping Yourself
or a Friend." Helpguide.org, October 2011. http://helpguide.org
/mental/depression_teen_teenagers.htm.
Centre for Clinical Interventions. "The ABC Analysis." *Back
from the Bluez*, 2008. www.cci.health.wa.gov.au/docs/BB-4-
Tho%20ABC%20Analysis.pdf.
Amanda Gardner. "Speed, Ecstasy Use Tied to Teen Depression." *Health*, April 18, 2012. http://news.health.com/2012
/04/18/speed-ecstasy-teen-depression.
Lynn Harbottle. *Healthy Eating and Depression*. Mental
Health Foundation, 2007. www.mentalhealth.org.uk/content
/assets/PDF/publications/healthy_eating_depression.pdf.
Mental Health America. "Depression in Teens," 2011. http://nmha
.org/index.cfm?objectid=C7DF950F-1372-4D20-C8B5BD8DF
DD94CF1.
Melinda Smith, Robert Segal, and Jeanne Segal. "Dealing with
Depression." Helpguide.org, October 2011. http://helpguide
.org/mental/depression_tips.htm.

Websites

About Teen Depression (www.about-teen-depression.com).
This site provides teens with a one-stop resource about depression, offering information about statistics, who is most
at risk for depression, how it is treated, and how to cope
with it, as well as links to a number of articles.
KidsHealth (www.kidshealth.org). A site that offers a wide
variety of health-related information for children and
teenagers, including a "Stress & Coping Center" and a search
engine that produces numerous articles about teen depression.

Psych Central Teenage Depression (http://psychcentral
.com/lib/2007/teenage-depression/all/1). This site is an excellent resource for teens who suffer from depression. It fea-
tures a depression quiz, a large collection of informative
articles, and a link to the *Depression on My Mind* blog.

Troubled Teen 101 (www.troubledteen101.com). Young people
will find valuable information on this site about depression
and related mental health issues.

Index

ABCD model, 79
Adolescent Depression
Awareness Program
(ADAP), 83–85
Alcohol, 46–47, 63, 74
American Academy of Child
and Adolescent Psychiatry
(AACAP), 18, 35, 49, 68
American Academy of
Pediatrics, 36
The Anatomy of Melancholy
(Burton), 13, *14*
Anhedonia, 32
Antidepressants, 53
APA (American Psychological
Association), 15

Bipolar disorder (manic
depression), 20–23
Brain
altered chemistry in, 30–32
effects of cortisol on, 34–35
endocrine system and, 34
epilepsy and, 41
exercise and, 57
magnetic stimulation of, 32,
33, 56
yoga and, 72–73
Bright light therapy
(phototherapy), 48, *48*
Burton, Robert, 13, 14
Butcher, James N., *39*

CBT. *See* Cognitive-behavioral
therapy
Centers for Disease Control
and Prevention (CDC), 18
Child abuse/neglect, 34–35
Chronic illness, 41
Cognitive-behavioral therapy
(CBT), 49–50, 53
in prevention programs, 78,
79
Coping
with depression, pets help
teens in, 67
rejecting unhealthy ways of,
74, 76
with stress, strategies for, 62
Cortisol, 34–35

Delusions, 26
Depression
genetics and, 28–30
hesitancy among teens to get
help for, 11, 44–46
hormones and, 34–35
illness coexisting with,
24–25, 27
normal teenage blues *vs.*, 8
pressure on teens to excel
and, 37–39, 41
prevalence among
teenagers, 23
psychotic, 26

Picture Credits

About the Author

Peggy J. Parks holds a bachelor of science degree from Aquinas College in Grand Rapids, Michigan, where she graduated magna cum laude. An author who has written more than one hundred educational books for children and young adults, Parks lives in Muskegon, Michigan, a town that she says inspires her writing because of its location on the shores of Lake Michigan.